WHITE STAR LINE

A PHOTOGRAPHIC HISTORY

Thos H Ismay
W Spithead
June 26 1897

WHITE STAR LINE

A PHOTOGRAPHIC HISTORY

JANETTE McCUTCHEON

AMBERLEY

Frontispiece: Thomas Henry Ismay, the founder of the White Star Line as we know it, was born in Maryport, Cumbria, in 1837 and became a shipowner and director of the National Line, before purchasing the bankrupt White Star Line in 1869. From his £1,000 initial investment grew one of the most famous of all shipping lines.

Right: Ceramic on the stocks, ready for launching, 11 December 1912.

First published 2006, revised edition 2013

Amberley Publishing
The Hill, Stroud
Gloucestershire, GL5 4EP
www.amberley-books.com

© Janette McCutcheon, 2013

The right of Janette McCutcheon to be identified as the Author of this work has been asserted in accordance with the Copyrights, Designs and Patents Act 1988.

British Library Cataloguing in Publication Data.
A catalogue record for this book is available from the British Library.

ISBN 978 1 4456 1801 2

Typesetting and origination by Amberley Publishing Plc
Printed in Great Britain

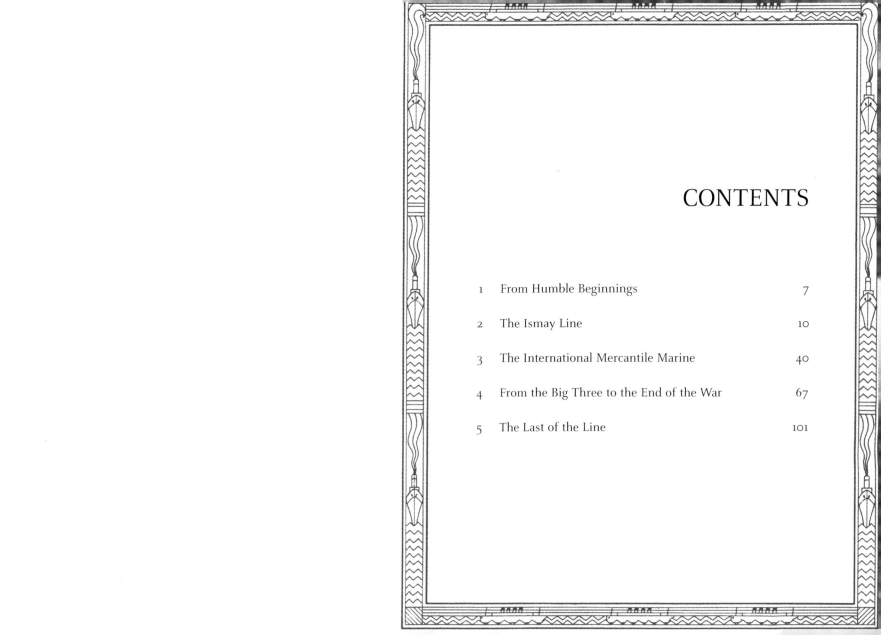

CONTENTS

Before Thomas Ismay purchased White Star, it had been one of the most well-known sailing ship lines to Australia from Liverpool. One of its most famous ships was *Red Jacket*, shown here on a postcard of *c.*1905. She was of wooden construction, 2,305 tons, and was built in 1853 in Rockland, Maine. She was wrecked in 1886 at Cape Verde when being used as a storage hulk.

Chapter 1

FROM HUMBLE BEGINNINGS

The White Star Line will always be associated with the Ismay family, but the line originated from very humble beginnings as Pilkington & Wilson Shipbrokers in 1845. John Pilkington and Henry Wilson set up a shipbroker's at North John Street, Liverpool in that year. The main trade of the company was to act as brokers for sailing ships on the American and Canadian transatlantic crossings in the days when sail still ruled the waves. After the success of their first charter, the *Elizabeth*, which sailed from Liverpool for Canada on 26 February 1846, the Pilkington & Wilson partnership continued chartering ships and went on to buy the *Iowa*, an 879-ton sailing barque, in 1849. In June of that year, they advertised the 'White Star Line of Boston Packets', taking cargo and emigrants to Charleston, New Orleans, New York and Boston. The two southern ports would have been supplying the Lancashire mills with cotton. It was most likely at this time that the company's flag came into being – a five pointed white star in a red background.

A few years later, in 1851 the Australian Gold Rush provided a unique opportunity for entrepreneurs and the Pilkington & Wilson White Star Line soon operated a roaring trade taking passengers to Australia.

From the first company-owned vessel, White Star expanded rapidly and advertising six ships sailing for Australia in an advert of 1 June 1852; *Phoenix*, *Dundonald*, *Bhurtpoor*, *Ellen*, *The Earl of Derby* and *Blanche*. *Bhurtpoor* was lost off the coast of Ireland and sank on 18 September 1852. The company still operated American packets too and H.T. Wilson ordered the *Jesse Munn* in 1852 for the American route and also the *Colonist*. In 1853, as an addition to the fleet, White Star then advertised a new-build named *Tayleur*. She was the one of the largest British-built ships at the time, certainly the largest ever built in Warrington, and cost £34,000. Disaster struck on the maiden sailing of the *Tayleur* when she was wrecked just off Dublin Bay. Her iron hull had stopped the compass working properly and she sailed onto the rocks of Lambay Island with 652 passengers and crew aboard. Over half, 380 souls, died as she sank.

The jewel of the early White Star fleet was *Red Jacket*. In the second half of 1854, she was the fastest sailing ship on the Australian run. In fact she was so fast, she could outstrip many of the steamships of the period on the route! Her journey time to Melbourne was a mere 67½ days.

The 1863 *Royal Standard*, on her return maiden voyage from Melbourne to Liverpool, encountered a huge iceberg, 600ft high, in dense fog and only luck saved the ship from disaster. Pushed against the monster berg by the wind, *Royal Standard* lost her main and mizzen masts followed by her foremast. Hard work on the part of the crew saw the wreckage cut away and the ship slowly escaped the berg. Fitted with steam engines, she limped to Rio de Janeiro where she was put under jury rig and sailed back home for more extensive repairs. It was not the last time that ice would play a part in the story of a ship of the line.

Changes to the board of White Star partnership happened over the next few years. In 1856, John Pilkington felt compelled to return to his family business (Pilkington Brothers); instead, Henry Wilson's brother-in-law, James Chambers, took Pilkington's place. The firm became known as H.T. Wilson & Chambers, managing the White Star Packets. In 1856, the line lost its Royal Mail contract to Cunard, with the advent of the steamship *Etna* on the Australian route.

The Australian route in this period proved to be very profitable for White Star. As long as passengers could be guaranteed a fast passage to Australia – otherwise the gold might disappear before they got there – then White Star had a 'licence to print money'. Chartering and owning ships throughout the late 1850s and early 1860s, the line seemed to be growing and expanding all the time. Trade with Australia was still good and the company chartered ships to sail to British Columbia for the gold rush there too.

In May 1863 the company acquired its first steamship, the *Albert Williams*, a barque of 505 tons. In November, the *Royal Standard* left Liverpool for Melbourne on her maiden voyage. She was built at Jarrow by Palmer Bros and was the first large steamship ordered for the line, being of 2.033grt and 225ft long. Propulsion was by a 165hp two cylinder steam engine and she carried three masts with a full set of sails. On the way to Australia, her captain, E.J. Allen, died and was replaced for the return voyage by captain G.H. Dorvell. On 21 March 1864 she sailed from Melbourne with ½ ton of gold on board but, on 4 April, she rammed an iceberg under full sail in thick fog. Crashing along the side of the 600ft high iceberg she was dismasted and her starboard side severely damaged. Still afloat, the ship's engine was started and she slowly sailed away from the berg, making Rio de Janeiro on 9 May where she was repaired.

In the same year, the company tried to amalgamate with the Eagle and Black Ball lines, but the merger was stopped when it was discovered that the owners of the three lines had tried to massage the share prices upwards for their own personal gain. Due to a great expansion, the White Star Line had run out of cash and tried to sell some of its ships to repay the debts which hung over the company. By 1865, H.T. Wilson and John Cunningham had become the principal shareholders of the company, although Chambers was still an active member of the partnership.

Owing almost £470,000 to the banks, the principal debtor of the company was the Royal Bank of Liverpool which promptly guaranteed its loans for another six years. Chambers was unhappy with the company's perilous finances and used the excuse that he disapproved of its advertising to resign from the firm in 1866. Henry Wilson was guaranteeing under penalty that passengers could make it to Australia in sixty-eight days. James Chambers set up his own company on the day he left White Star. Wilson and John Cunningham were left with White Star. Despite their debts, the company stayed afloat until 1867 when, after the collapse of the Royal Bank of Liverpool, the line, owing £527,000, followed it into receivership. The fleet was sold to pay the debts. H.T. Wilson, now a broken man, was left with only the name and goodwill of the company.

The White Star Line faced a very uncertain future. Wilson died of stomach cancer, in much reduced circumstances, in November 1869, aged only forty-four. John Pilkington died in 1890 in Birkenhead. In late 1867, Wilson had sold the goodwill, name and flag of the White Star Line. One man, a director of the transatlantic National Line, and shipowner in his own right, the Maryport-born Thomas Henry Ismay, had the vision to buy the bankrupt line and soon White Star Line ships were sailing again to Australia.

Chapter 2

THE ISMAY LINE

T.H. Ismay & Co. already had a fleet of sailing ships when, on 18 January 1868, Thomas Ismay purchased the White Star Line for £1,000. Then, aged 30, this young entrepreneur set about building up a fleet of the most modern vessels on the seas. T.H. Ismay had great plans for the line and over the course of the next three years, he was to build a fleet of steamships to rival the best on the Atlantic run.

After talks with Gustav Schwabe, the Liverpool ship financier, a plan was devised. If Ismay were to have his ships built by Schwabe's nephew's company – Harland & Wolff in Belfast – then Schwabe would guarantee financial backing for the ships. On 6 September 1869, Ismay registered a new company as The Oceanic Steam Navigation Company, although it was to be more commonly known as the White Star Line. Amongst the official shareholders were Gustav Schwabe, E.J. Harland, Gustav W. Wolff and, of course, T.H. Ismay. Four steam packets were immediately ordered from the Belfast yard – *Oceanic*, *Atlantic*, *Baltic* and *Republic*. The company was still running their White Star Packets on the profitable Australia run.

The year 1870 was a great year for White Star. Firstly, William Imrie, who had been an apprentice with Thomas Ismay, joined the line to manage the group's sailing ships. He transferred the assets of Imrie, Tomlinson, his father's company, to T.H. Ismay and the company was renamed as Ismay, Imrie & Co. Then the keel of yard no.73 was laid at Belfast. This was the keel of the *Oceanic* – the first of the first four ships ordered from Harland & Wolff. There was speculation that this ship was to sail on the England-Australia route, but her bunkers suggested a more challenging occupation – the North Atlantic route. Of course, as a director of the National Line, Ismay was no stranger to the transatlantic route.

The North Atlantic route from Liverpool was extremely competitive. Already on it were Cunard, Guion, National and Inman Lines. The route started mainly as a mail service between England and America/Canada, but as time progressed, the trade turned to passengers. Many sailing packet passengers had been disgruntled at the inefficiency, danger and primitive conditions encountered when travelling on the sailing packets and emigrant ships, and turned to the steamships, with their properly trained crews, better living quarters (and food) and sailing schedules. These passengers were even willing to pay more for the privilege. As the first-class passenger volume increased, the companies then looked

Right: The first White Star Line steamship, built under the management of T.H. Ismay, was the *Oceanic*, of 1871. Built in Belfast, she was a revolution in steamship technology and far ahead of almost every other ship that had preceded her. Each new White Star ship was to continue this trend. This view from the late 1870s shows her near sister *Celtic* in the Mersey, off Liverpool.

Below: Many people do not realise that sail was still as important in the 1870s steamships and here *Oceanic* is shown under full sail. Using a combination of sail and steam she used about 58 tons of coal per day and she had a potential top speed of 14.5kt.

First Steamer of White Star Line "Oceanic" 1871

With so many new ships added to the fleet in the first four years, *Oceanic* was declared surplus in 1875. She was transferred to the Occidental & Oriental SS Co. and chartered from White Star for their San Francisco-Yokohama-Hong Kong service. She is shown here at Amoy in 1879. She sailed on this route for twenty years and was then scrapped after it was decided that refitting her with new engines was uneconomic.

at another way of expanding their income and realized that there was a steady stream of emigrants, all wanting passage to the New World. While first class passengers took up quite a bit of space and required all sorts of luxuries, such as nice cabins, spectacular public rooms and good quality food, lots of emigrants could be packed into a small, cramped space, with basic food and facilities. More money could be made out of emigrant passengers than any other class of passenger, just because of the sheer numbers of people traveling one way to North America.

The competition of the North Atlantic was fierce and the companies had different policies for their vessels. Cunard insisted on 'safety, followed by excellent service', whereas other lines ensured that their ships were the fastest on the route. Mostly, it was the fastest, most luxurious ships that attracted the first class clientele, while the emigrants wanted to be on a safe, fast ship. The emigrants perceived that the bigger the ship the safer it was; also the more funnels the ship had, the more power it had. Quite often, even the basic facilities on these large liners were more luxurious than emigrants had ever encountered and after six days of travelling, they didn't want to get off! It is also forgotten that the passenger ships also carried huge volumes of cargo both ways across the Atlantic too. In 1870 the National Line carried almost 400,000 tons of cargo.

The new White Star ships were to be a revelation on the Atlantic. Built to a new and revolutionary design, they were to set the standards for the next thirty years. The design introduced long, sleek hulls, proper decks, first-class accommodation amidships, steerage aft, and novelties such as baths, electricity and even double bed bridal suites. The relationship with Harland & Wolff, with every ship built on a cost-plus-profit basis, ensured that only the finest liners were built for Ismay, Imrie's White Star Line. *Oceanic* set a new benchmark for luxury, and one the other lines had to match. She sailed triumphantly into Liverpool on 26 February 1871 as the finest ship afloat.

Despite the luxurious appointments and striking new design, passenger traffic was not forthcoming for the maiden voyage of White Star's first transatlantic ocean liner. As the *Oceanic* left Liverpool on her maiden voyage on 2 March 1871, bound for New York, she was only carrying 64 passengers. Cunard's rather older and much more primitive *Calabria*, on a parallel sailing, carried 300 passengers. The maiden voyage was postponed after *Oceanic*'s bearings overheated of Holyhead and she returned to Liverpool for repairs. She left for New York again on 16 March and sailed into New York where she was opened to the public. 50,000 traipsed around her admiring her luxury fittings and her solid, new design. Shortly afterwards, in June, *Atlantic* entered service, followed by *Baltic* (I) in September. *Baltic* was to have originally been called *Pacific*, but the name was considered unlucky after the sinking of the Collins Line vessel of that name.

Breaking into the North Atlantic trade was difficult for White Star. To offset this problem, they also diversified their sailing schedules into other areas such as the transpacific route, with numerous of their ships chartered to the Occidental & Oriental Steam Ship Co., a business relationship that was to last twenty years.

When *Republic* (I) entered service in 1871, White Star began ordering pairs of ships to compete on the North Atlantic route. Their first major victory was with the 3,888 ton *Adriatic*. After she took the record for the fastest transatlantic voyage from the Cunard liner *Scotia*, the public began to take notice of this new upstart line. White Star felt that a different marketing strategy had to be adopted from their competitors – they decided to go for luxurious accommodation, with a hint of speed, a policy that was to work for the remainder of the line's existence.

Above: One of the first four ships, *Atlantic*, was wrecked at Marr's Rock, Meaghers Island, off Nova Scotia, on 1 April 1873 while on her nineteenth voyage. Of the 931 on board, 585 perished, including all but one of the seventy-eight children on board.

Opposite left: An 1870s advert showing *Britannic* or *Germanic* under sail and steam, heading for the USA.

Opposite right: An 1886 advert, interestingly listing all of the captains of the ships. Thursday was the traditional sailing day for ships of the White Star Line at the time.

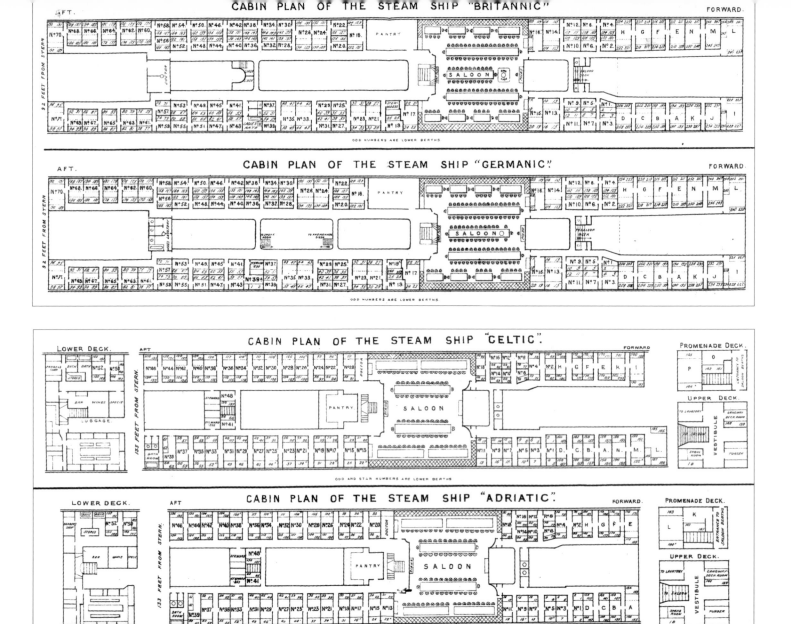

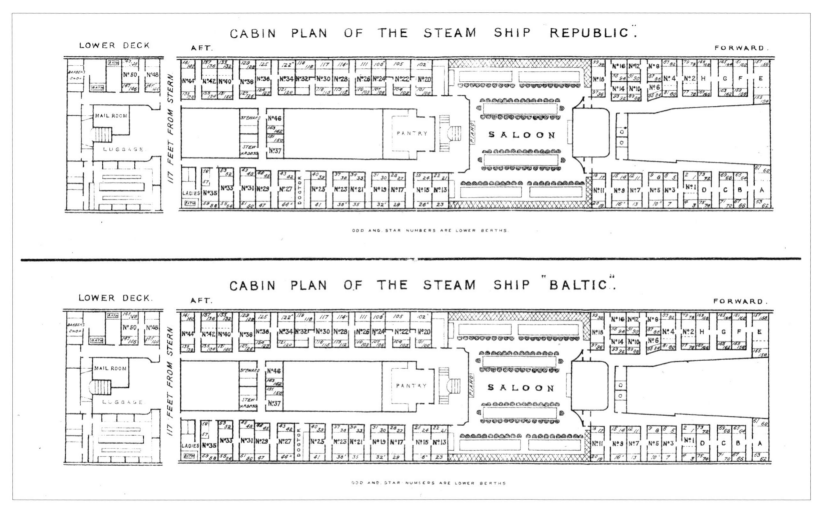

Above and opposite page: Life on board was quite luxurious for Saloon passengers with prices ranging from £12 to £22 for one way passage. *Britannic* and *Germanic* were the largest ships of the fleet at just over 5,000grt each in 1886, albeit already almost twelve years old.

WINE CARD.

NOTICE.

Passengers will oblige by ordering, at Luncheon, the Wine they may require for Dinner.

LIST OF WINES AND SPIRITS.

		PRICES.	
		QUART.	PINT.
CHAMPAGNE	GIESLER'S FIRST QUALITY... ... HEIDSIECK'S CARTE BLANCHE... MOET & CHANDON'S WHITE DRY, SPARKLING SILLERY..... ... G. H. MUMM & Co.'s FIRST QUALITY PERRIER JOUET & Co.'s CUVEE DE RESERVE .... WATCHER'S EXTRA CUVEE	7/6	4/-
SHERRY	VINO DE PASTO } GONZALEZ .... DUCHA ... . }	5/-	
CLARET	MARGAUX ..... MEDOC	5/- 3/-	3/- 1/6
PORT	....	4/-	
STILL HOCK			
SPARKLING HOCK	}	5/-	3/-
SPARKLING MOSELLE	....	5/-	3/-
SPARKLING BURGUNDY	....	6/-	3/-
MADEIRA	....	6/-	
		BOTTLE.	GLASS.
BRANDY.—HENNESSY'S AND MARTELL'S......		6/-	6d.
WHISKY.—IRISH AND SCOTCH		5/-	6d.
OLD TOM and HOLLAND'S GIN		5/-	6d.
LIQUEURS.—CHARTREUSE, MARASCHINO, AND CURAÇOA........................		10/-	6d.

Ale, Porter, Apollinaris, and Congress Water, English Seltzer, Ginger Ale, Lemonade and Soda Water, 6d. per bottle; Cigars, 6d. each.

ALL, EXCEPT BOTTLES OF WINES AND SPIRITS, TO BE PAID FOR ON DELIVERY.

The Purser is directed to Present and Collect the Wine Bills against Passengers on the day previous to the Ship's arrival.

Above: In the late 1870s, the line published a guide to its fleet and its services. Illustrated throughout with colour lithographs, the guide showed accommodation on board the vessels. This is the Grand Saloon, amidships, on either *Germanic* or *Britannic*.

Left: Wine could be purchased by either the quart or the pint on board.

Below: White Star and its associated shipping lines could truly offer a transatlantic and transpacific route by 1880, as well as routes to Australia, New Zealand and China.

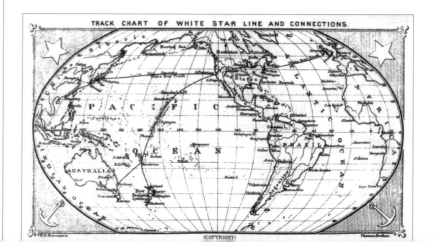

Right: Even from an early age, grand staircases were a notable feature of White Star vessels. This one, on board *Germanic* or *Britannic*, was the main route to most parts of the ship for its saloon passengers.

Below left: Note the specially designed tables in the Smoking Saloon of *Germanic* or *Britannic*, with cutouts to prevent glasses and pint pots being spilled in rough seas. It is hard to believe nowadays that ships would have dedicated smoking rooms. They were out of bounds for ladies too.

Below right: Unless the weather was good, little time was spent out of doors on the seven-ten day crossing. This view looks down from amidships to the stern on the starboard side of *Germanic* or *Britannic*.

New routes to South America were opened up with the main competition on this route being the Pacific Steam Navigation Company. *Republic* (I) sailed via Cape Horn to Valparaiso to inaugurate White Star's South American route. White Star purchased off the stocks two new steamships, *Asiatic* (I) and *Tropic* (I), for the South American service but both were sold in 1873, with less than two year's service for the line. Soon White Star purchased the *Gaelic* (I) and *Belgic* (I). The order for both these ships was placed by the Pacific Steam Navigation Company, but White Star bought them on the stocks. Unfortunately, the South American route was never a success but, despite the failure of the route for the steamships, the company's sailing vessels made regular voyages to South America.

The White Star success on the North Atlantic route seemed unstoppable when the *Baltic* (I) took the transatlantic record on an eastbound voyage in January 1873 at an average speed of 15.09kt. By now, the company was a major player on the North Atlantic Service, with the speedy and luxurious ships making them a leading carrier.

A major disaster, and not their last either, occurred on 1 April 1873, when the liner *Atlantic* was en-route from Liverpool to New York. During stormy weather, she tried to change course and make for Halifax, as her fuel supplies were running short. Unfortunately, she ran aground at speed onto Marr's Rock, Meaghers Island, near Halifax, Nova Scotia, and was wrecked. Of the 920 souls on board, 588 were lost.

In 1874, as the steamship service to South America ceased, a pair of new ships were being introduced to the North Atlantic run; *Britannic* (I) and *Germanic*. True to the Harland & Wolff principle of being at the forefront of technology, *Britannic* was the first ship to be fitted with an adjustable propeller shaft, which increased thrust. Although revolutionary, this was not a great success and it was taken out after just nine voyages.

The two new North Atlantic liners, *Germanic* and *Britannic* were a huge success. They competed against each other for the fastest crossings of the North Atlantic. Finally, Guion Line's *Alaska* took the westbound transatlantic record from *Germanic* but White Star had most definitely arrived and its two newest ships were acknowledged as the finest afloat.

The Pacific routes were not forgotten, and in 1881, the new *Arabic* (I) and *Coptic* were added to the fleet. 1883 saw *Ionic* (I) and *Doric* (I) start a service to New Zealand (this was operated jointly with Shaw, Savill & Albion,). The link with Shaw, Savill & Albion brokered in 1883 was to last until the 1930s. More importantly, the two ships were the very first constructed by Harland & Wolff out of steel. After this, the *Belgic* (II) and the *Gaelic* were built for the San Francisco-Yokohama-Hong Kong route.

Alaska's reign on the fastest North Atlantic crossing was not for long, as Cunard's *Etruria* took the record away from her. *Etruria's* sister, *Umbria*, then took the coveted title. Soon White Star responded by building two new ships, *Teutonic* and *Majestic*, in 1889 and 1890 respectively. *Teutonic* was converted to an armed merchant cruiser upon her maiden arrival in Liverpool and sped straight for Spithead for the Naval Review, complete with eight 4.7in guns. She then rushed back to Liverpool for her maiden voyage on 7 August. *Teutonic* was the next White Star vessel to capture the Blue Riband when, in 1891, she took the westbound record from the Inman Line.

A new build for the New Zealand service was *Gothic*, which made her maiden voyage in 1893. She was the largest vessel at the time to sail into the Port of London and made her first trip to Wellington, New Zealand in a record 37½ days. Later she was joined by *Delphic* (I) in 1897.

Always seeing an opening for new markets, White Star constructed a series of cattle carriers, used to carry livestock from the USA to Europe. Mostly with bovine names, the most infamous of these was *Naronic*, which disappeared in February 1893 while crossing the Atlantic on only her seventh voyage. *Naronic* was the only White Star ship to go missing with all hands. To this day no-one knows how she disappeared,

Steerage was much more cramped with men and women sleeping in dormitories. Public space was nowhere near as luxurious as that of the Saloon passengers, but there was often music and dancing with the entertainment being sourced from the passengers themselves. The food was also much simpler but that did not stop some people becoming ill with all of the rich food.

although there were two lifeboats found after the loss and some bottles with messages supposedly from the ship– most of which were proved to be fake. Another, *Runic*, was sold and, during the First World War, rammed a French ammunition ship in Halifax harbour, Nova Scotia, with devastating effect. Over 10,000 were killed or seriously injured and half of Halifax was destroyed in the resulting explosion.

By the mid-1890s, trade on the Atlantic was remarkably different from only a decade before. Lines like the Guion Line had disappeared in 1894, the National Line made its last passenger sailing that year too and the Inman Line had transferred its ships to Southampton and to the American Line in 1893, leaving only Cunard and White Star as the dominant Liverpool lines. In 1896 Ismay, Imrie was to sell its last sailing vessel and William Imrie retired.

Despite the loss of these famous names on the transatlantic routes, the trade in the North Atlantic had a new challenger – the German Norddeutscher Lloyd Line. Their new ship *Kaiser Wilhelm der Grosse* easily snatched the Blue Riband from Britain and gave the new German nation supremacy of the seas. The *Kaiser Wilhelm der Grosse* was also the first four-funnelled ship and it was generally associated at the time by the traveling public that the more funnels, the faster and safer the ship.

By now, White Star was turning to a new philosophy – moderate speed, comfort, punctuality and reliability. While other ships were travelling at dangerous speeds in stormy weather, White Star decided to give their passengers a comfortable ride. The ships might not make port in record-breaking time, but if their passengers had a (fairly) comfortable journey in the most luxurious ships, they were more likely to return, than

Right: Safety was paramount and the ships were constructed with a specially-designed fire-fighting pump system that could extinguish fires in the bunkers.

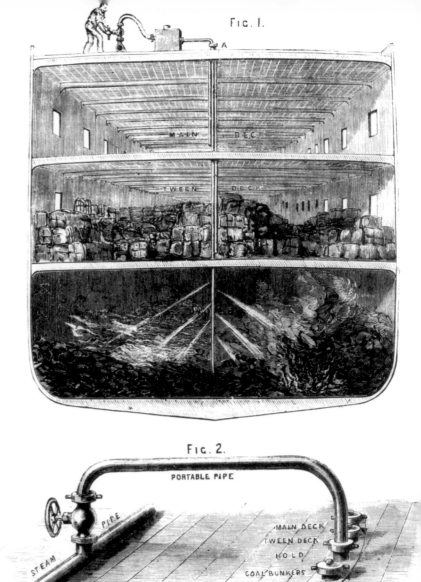

At Neptune Street, Liverpool, the company had its own engineering and repair shops, capable of fabricating and repairing all sorts of damage inflicted by Atlantic storms.

Britannic in the Mersey in the late 1870s. She was to be withdrawn from service in 1899 but went on to become a Boer War troop transport and was not scrapped until 1903.

Above: *Runic,* sister of *Cufic*, was sold to become the Norwegian *Imo.* After a collision in Halifax with the SS *Mont Blanc*, the latter ship exploded, causing huge damage to Halifax, Nova Scotia.

Left and below left: Two views of *Germanic* at the Landing Stage in Liverpool, photographed from the Isle of Man Steam Packet Co.'s berth sometime in the 1880s.

Below right: Britannic's funnels were extended in 1895 while the once-open bridge was closed in.

Above left: Germanic took the Blue Riband of the Atlantic in July 1875 and, with her sister, was recognised as the finest liner afloat at that the time.

Above right: In 1885 a new *Gaelic* was launched, and she made her maiden voyage from Liverpool to New York in May. On 10 November 1885 she sailed from San Francisco on the Occidental & Oriental transpacific service. In 1904 she sailed for the UK and a refit in Belfast then sold to the Pacific Steam Navigation Co. for further service as *Callao*. In 1907, she was broken up at Briton Ferry, Wales.

Below left: Adriatic or *Celtic* in the Mersey, *c*.1880.

Below right: Cufic, the first of White Star's cattle carriers, was another revolutionary ship from Harland & Wolff and was the first White Star ship fitted with triple-expansion steam engines. She carried general cargo to the USA and brought up to 1,000 livestock back to the UK. Her sister was *Runic*, built in 1889.

Above, left and right: Showing their propensity for building in pairs, the next two cattle carriers were *Nomadic* and *Tauric*, both built in 1891. *Nomadic* was the first White Star ship requisitioned for Boer War trooping use. In 1904 both ships were transferred within International Mercantile Marine to the Dominion Line. *Nomadic* was renamed as *Cornishman* in 1904 and sold to F. Leyland in 1921, then broken up in 1926 at Lelant, Cornwall. *Tauric* was renamed *Welshman* and broken up at Bo'ness, West Lothian, three years later than her sister.

Below left: In 1892, *Bovic* was launched. She was almost identical to the ill-fated *Naronic*, lost with all hands in 1893. In 1914 she undertook Manchester-New York sailings and her masts were cut down so she could transit the Manchester Ship Canal. In 1922, she transferred to the Leyland Line and was scrapped in 1928. She is shown here at Salford, Manchester.

Below right: Cevic was the second to last of the cattle carriers built. In 1908, when the cattle service stopped, she was transferred to the Australian route via the Cape initially then via the Suez Canal. In 1914 she was converted into a dummy battleship, to confuse the Germans, and sailed for some time pretending to be HMS *Queen Mary*. In September 1915 she was decommissioned and the gun turrets and other paraphernalia of war removed. In 1916 she was converted into an oil tanker, the open decks making the conversion simple, and she survived until 1933. She was broken up in Genoa.

Above left: At 10,077grt *Georgic* was larger than many ocean liners but was designed to carry livestock. When built she was the largest livestock carrier in the world. On 10 December 1916, she was en route from Philadelphia, carrying 1,200 horses and 10,000 barrels of oil, when she was sunk by the German commerce raider *Moewe*.

Above right: With a slender 9.7:1 hull ratio, *Teutonic* was an extremely beautiful ship, as this side profile shows.

Below left: Built as an armed merchant cruiser, *Teutonic* entered service in 1889. She is shown here when attending the Spithead Naval Review, complete with her 4.7in guns. She had strengthened hull plating as well as decks and was designed to an Admiralty specification.

Below right: Shown here in the Mersey, just off Egremont, *Teutonic* shows off her slim lines. In 1907, she was transferred to Southampton for the new White Star service to New York. In September 1914, she was taken up as an armed merchant cruiser and fitted with larger 6in guns. She survived the war but was broken up in 1921.

Above left: Teutonic being coaled at Southampton. The dust sheets covering the promenade deck were to prevent dust covering the passenger accommodation. She desperately needs a paint and freshen up in this view.

Above right: Teutonic was also used as a troopship in 1918, carrying 1,500 soldiers from the UK to Alexandria, in which guise she is shown here. Her promenade deck is boarded up with small portholes only – this was done to prevent shrapnel from shells killing or maiming the troops.

Above left: Being attended by the tug *A.J. Barrett, Teutonic's* sister *Majestic* is shown leaving New York in the 1900s. *Majestic* was also a Blue Riband winner, taking the westbound record in July 1891. Photographed sometime after 1903, when she was refitted with two masts only, she also made the transition to Southampton for the new express service in 1907.

Above right: In November 1911, *Majestic* was relegated to reserve and mothballed at Bidston Dock, Birkenhead. The wisdom of this move was shown barely six months later when *Titanic* sank. On 14 January 1914, she made her final sailing to New York and was sold soon after for scrap.

Above left: Majestic in the Mersey, with the passenger tender *Magnetic* to her starboard.

Above right: Entering Southampton Water for the first time in June 1907, *Majestic* made her first sailing from the port on 26 June.

if they had been seasick! In the emigrant trade too, word would spread that White Star liners gave comfortable and trouble-free crossings, which also meant more custom for the line.

For almost a decade White Star had constructed no new large passenger liners, but that was to change at the turn of the twentieth century. With the advent of the *Kaiser Wilhelm der Grosse*, it was obvious that White Star, to retain its supremacy of the Atlantic, would have to build new tonnage.

Again, White Star was to stun the shipping world with a liner of such opulence and magnificence that she was fêted as a wonder of the world. When *Oceanic* came into service in 1899, she was the first ship to eclipse the length (but not tonnage) of the *Great Eastern* of 1858. *Oceanic* could maintain a speed of 19 knots, which gave her a comfortable 6 day crossing time. Although not as fast as the crack German liners, she was by far and

After being sold for scrap, *Majestic* sailed for Morecambe, dressed overall in flags, where she arrived on 5 May. Opened to the public, thousands swarmed over her before she was broken up later that year. Here she is on the day she arrived for breaking.

Within a few weeks, *Majestic* was high and dry and the serious work of dismantling her began, but not before many of her fixtures and fittings had been sold off.

Above, left and right: In 1893, the *Gothic* was delivered for the joint service with Shaw, Savill & Albion to New Zealand and was, at the time, the biggest ship on the route and the largest ship to enter the Port of London when she made her maiden call there. These two views show just how luxurious she was.

away the most luxurious liner in the world. Plans were made for a sister ship, to be called *Olympic* (I), but they were cancelled upon the death of T.H. Ismay on 23 November 1899. It was perhaps a co-incidence that Ismay had died as a larger ship was already on the drawing board. The *Celtic* (II) was the first ship in the world to weigh more than 20,000 tons, thus the White Star Line already had one ship that was longer than the *Great Eastern*, and now one that was heavier! Although the largest ship on the ocean at the time, *Celtic* wasn't designed to be operated at anywhere near full speed as it was more economical to run her at a steady 16 knots.

New ships for the Liverpool-Australia service were delivered too. Named *Afric*, *Medic* and *Persic*, these ships were used for troop transport during the Boer War and requisitioned during the First World War.

With the death of T.H. Ismay, his eldest son J. Bruce Ismay took control of the company. The line was to remain independent for only a short while. This was a period of consolidation in the shipping world, mainly caused by the actions of a single man, John Pierpoint Morgan, an American financier. Interesting times lay ahead for J. Bruce Ismay and White Star.

Top: *Afric* leaving Melbourne on 17 July 1913.

Above: *Gothic* in the Thames off Tilbury *c.*1905.

Right: An 1898 poster advertising the arrivals of White Star vessels.

White Star Line

BRITANNIC arrived at 2.44 A. M. this morning. Passage 7 days, 17 hours, 44 minutes. Sails for Queenstown and Liverpool next Wednesday, Sept. 7, at noon. Saloon Rates from $75 upwards. No Second Cabin. Third Class rates to Queenstown, Liverpool, London, Glasgow, Belfast and Derry, $25.50; Bristol, $28.20; Cardiff, $28.00; Gothenborg, Christiania, Bergen, Stavanger, Copenhagen, &c., $30.50; Stockholm, Hango and Helsingfors, $33.50; Hamburg and Bremen, $33; Antwerp and Rotterdam, $35. Capetown, $69.50—Single men only. Closed Cabins, $85.50. Agents will please remember to endorse on the tickets and stubs the fact that they have collected the War Tax, and also to use a separate ticket for each adult, Third Class. Two children may be placed on same ticket.

GERMANIC arrived at Queenstown at 6 p. m. Wedday. Passage 6 days and 23 hours.

NEW ZEALAND.

The White Star Steamer "DELPHIC," will sail from London to New Zealand direct, on September 29th, Intending passengers can connect with this Steamer by any sailing up to, and including "GERMANIC," September 21st from New York.

WHITE STAR LINE.

New York, September 2, '98.

Above left: Gothic in the Thames, off Gravesend.

Above right: In June 1906, returning from New Zealand to England, *Gothic*'s cargo of cotton caught fire as she approached Land's End in Cornwall. With the fire getting worse she was beached off Plymouth and the fire eventually put out. Repairs took eight months and she returned to service for the Red Star Line as the *Gothland*, her luxurious interiors so damaged that she was rebuilt as an emigrant ship. In 1926 she was broken up at Bo'ness, Scotland.

Opposite page, clockwise from top left:

Romanic at Genoa. Built as *New England* in 1898 for the Dominion Line, she was transferred into White Star service in 1903 and made White Star's first sailing on the Liverpool-Boston route in November of that year. Then she inaugurated the Boston-Mediterranean service in December, on which service she is shown here.

Romanic at the Azores. She was popular with Americans taking a long cruise to Europe. In 1912 she was sold to the Allan Line to become their *Scandinavian* and laid up in 1922. She was scrapped a year later in Hamburg.

White Star ships laid up in the Gladstone dock, Liverpool, *c.*1905. *Oceanic* lies at the stern of *Cretic*, which is boarded up.

Medic at Sydney, most likely on her maiden voyage in 1899.

Cymric was originally intended to be a cattle carrier but White Star's plans changed during construction and she was built as a third-class emigrant carrier. In February 1898 she made her maiden voyage from Liverpool to New York. Always very profitable due to her huge cargo capacity and economical engines, she made sailings as a Boer War transport, and afterwards was placed on the Liverpool-Boston route. On 29 April 1916 she was torpedoed by U20, the same submarine that had sunk the *Lusitania* almost a year before. Remaining afloat until 9 May, five people lost their lives in the attack and while abandoning ship.

R.M.S. "ROMANIC" LYING OFF PONTA DELGADA, AZORES.

Above left: Medic in the Mersey, dressed overall in flags. *Medic* and her sisters, *Afric* and *Persic*, were all designed for the Cape service to Australia. *Medic* had a long life with White Star and was sold in 1928 and converted into a whale factory ship. On 11 September 1942, she was sunk by U-608 while serving as an oil tanker in Ministry of War Transport service.

Above right: Persic, probably photographed in Belfast Lough, just before being handed over by Harland & Wolff to her owners on 16 November 1899. On her maiden voyage her rudder stock broke and she was stranded at Cape Town until a new one was shipped out from Belfast. While painted in Norman Wilkinson's dazzle paint camouflage scheme she was torpedoed off the Scillies carrying almost 3,000 American troops. Thankfully, she was beached and repaired. In 1927 she left the Mersey for Rotterdam on her final voyage to the breakers.

Opposite above left: The voyage to Australia could be long, almost forty days, and when crossing the Equator a ceremony was always performed for those who had never been so far south. Here, some of the crew of *Persic* are dressed for the day's festivities on 9 July 1913.

Opposite below left: Sunday Inspection aboard the *Medic* on 3 July 1910.

Opposite above and below right: These shots aboard *Persic* were taken while crossing the Equator at Christmas in 1912.

Above and below: Oceanic was White Star's first ship and it was only fitting that the finest ship of the nineteenth century also carried the same name. Costing £750,000 the second *Oceanic* was the first ship to exceed the length of Isambard Kingdom Brunel's SS *Great Eastern.*

Above: A sister ship, to be named *Olympic*, was planned but never constructed. This was due to the death of T.H. Ismay and to the plans already in progress for an even bigger vessel. This view shows *Oceanic* at the Landing Stage Liverpool, in her first year of service.

Right: Shown here at Belfast, *Oceanic* left there on 26 August 1899 for her sea trials. On 30 August 1899 she arrived in Liverpool and was opened to the press and public. Her maiden voyage was on 6 September and she reached New York at a speed of 19.57kt. When running at top speed, she was prone to vibration.

Chapter 3

THE INTERNATIONAL MERCANTILE MARINE

John Pierpoint Morgan made his money financing railroad construction in the USA and his business empire controlled many of the railways on the eastern seaboard. He had a plan to buy up as many shipping lines as he could that were trading on the North Atlantic and create a near monopoly on the trade. He could then decide rates for transatlantic trade and this would ensure that his shipping lines would always be profitable By the time he acquired White Star, he already owned the Red Star, Dominion, Atlantic Transport, Leyland and American Lines and had shareholdings in many others. His company, named the International Mercantile Marine (IMM), was one of the largest shipping companies in the world at the time, owning and operating numerous fleets of ocean liners and cargo ships.

Morgan, after buying up the small lines, looked at the larger lines. Approaches were made to the four dominant transatlantic lines, Hamburg Amerika, Norddeutscher Lloyd, Cunard and White Star. The first two declined to sell but did enter into trade agreements with IMM, Cunard steadfastly refused to sell and White Star initially rebuked the advances. Morgan initiated a trade war by cutting rates on his fleets and took much

of the custom from the other lines. It hit White Star hard and, eventually, Ismay met with Morgan to discuss a possible merger.

The British Government tried to intervene in the takeover of White Star because it wanted the line to remain British (if not, it would not have enough troop-carrying capacity in the event of war). As a result, it was agreed between Morgan and the British Government that White Star remained a British Line, would run under the British Flag and have British officers and crew.

The cash injection from IMM put the ailing White Star Line on its feet. Soon after this, IMM made another bid for Cunard, the remaining main British shipping line. Cunard was not enthusiastic about this proposed takeover and instead approached the British Government to see if it could help them. The government devised a deal whereby, if Cunard were to remain loyal to the British flag, and provide troop-carrying capacity in the event of war, then it would help them build newer and larger ships which could hold their own against IMM ships on the North Atlantic. Cunard agreed and remained independent.

With the new backing from IMM, White Star embarked on a new building programme. *Cedric* arrived only two months into the new

White Star Line.

MAJESTIC arrived at I A. M. to-day. Sails for Queenstown and Liverpool next Wednesday, May 7th, at **12 Noon.** Saloon rates from **$100** up. Second Saloon from $45 up. Third Class Rates to Queenstown, Liverpool, London, Glasgow, Belfast and Derry, $29.50; Bristol, $32.20; Cardiff, $32.00; Gothenburg, Christiania, Bergen, Stavanger, Copenhagen, &c., $34.50; Stockholm, Hango and Helsingfors, $37.50; Hamburg, Antwerp, Rotterdam and Bremen, $33.00; Oswieczim, $37.15; Oderberg, $37.00.

TEUTONIC arrived at Queenstown yesterday.

GERMANIC sails from Queenstown to-day, and will be due to arrive here on Thursday, May 8th. Sails May 14th at noon. Saloon rates from **$75 up.**

CELTIC sailed from Queenstown last Saturday, and will be due to arrive here next Saturday evening. She brings 400 Saloon and **Two Thousand** Third Class passengers. The latter, we hope will land on Sunday morning. The Celtic sails from here Friday, May 9th at **7 A. M.** Passengers embark Thursday night. Saloon rates from $99 up. Second Saloon $45 up. As this Steamer has **very superior** accommodation for Third Class passengers we trust our Agents will endeavor to secure some passengers. There are desirable accommodations vacant in both First and Second Saloon this sailing.

WHITE STAR LINE.

New York, May 1st, 1902.

TWIN SCREW STEAMER "OCEANIC."

2ND CLASS.

JULY 25TH. 1911

.˙. **MENU.** .˙.

GREEN PEA SOUP

FILLETS OF FLOUNDER

CAPILOTADE OF CHICKEN

ROAST PORK. SAGE & ONION SAUCE
RIBS OF BEEF. YORKSHIRE PUDDING

CHOPPED CABBAGE   BOILED RICE
BROWNED & BOILED POTATOES

- SALAD -

VICTORIA PUDDING   BLANC MANGE
AMERICAN ICE CREAM

FRUIT   NUTS

CHEESE   BISCUITS   COFFEE

Above left: A 1902 advertising poster giving the sailings and arrivals. Interestingly, *Celtic* was carrying over 2,000 emigrants. They would be landed a whole day after the First Class passengers and transported directly to Ellis Island for processing.

Above right: Typical fare in second class. This menu was intended to be used as a postcard afterwards. Second-class from New York to Liverpool was $45, and first-class was $99 upwards, depending on cabin.

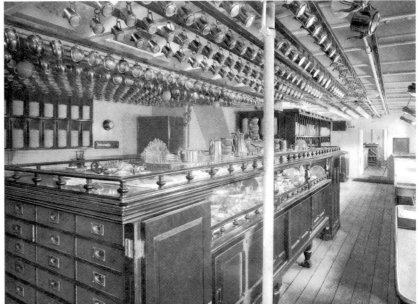

Above left: Looking down onto the engine room. *Oceanic* had twin triple expansion engines operating her two propeller shafts. She had fifteen double-ended boilers which operated at 192psi.

Above right: Third class was rather more primitive. This is the Smoking Room. Note the spittoons on the floor.

Right: The pantry for the Saloon passengers. This view shows just some of the silverplate.

Above left: In 1900, Harland & Wolff built the last two of the five ship monthly Australian service vessels. They were *Runic* (shown here) and *Suevic*. *Runic* was launched on 25 October 1900 and made her maiden voyage in January 1901. The hull design was identical to *Afric* but the poop deck was extended, giving 12,482grt, almost 600 more than *Afric*.

Above right: Runic in the Mersey.

Runic sailed out of White Star service and became the *New Sevilla*, a whaling factory ship. This stern view shows the ramp used to haul whales aboard the vessel. She was torpedoed off Malin Head, Galway, by U-138 on 20 October 1940, while en route to Antarctica. After floating for twenty hours, she sank thirty miles from the coast of Ireland.

WHITE STAR LINE.
TO
South Africa and Australia.

TWIN SCREW STEAMSHIP "SUEVIC."

Above left: *Suevic* had the much more interesting life of the pair, and was also the largest of the five vessels on the service. On 17 March 1907, inward bound to Plymouth, with 382 passengers on board, she ran aground on Stag Rock, the Manacles. Going ashore at full speed, 13.5kt, she stuck fast. The ship, however, was not terminally damaged and attempts were made to lighten her by removing the cargo and floating her off. These proved unsuccessful and it was decided to attempt something that had never been done before.

Above right: A letterhead from *Suevic*.

Right: Lifeboats raced to the aid of *Suevic* and her passengers were accommodated all over Devon and Cornwall. Some managed to find shelter in Hope, Devon.

HOPE VILLAGE WHERE THE RESCUED PASSENGERS WERE SHELTERED

Beaufort St
Chelsea
27/3/07

Dear Madam

I wish to thank you, for your Kindness to my wife at the Time of the Wreck of the Suevic. I would have written before but my wife has been Ill, & my arm sore, from a Dislocated Shoulder, & Relic of the Wreck

Yours Truly
Jno Cogdon

P.S. We met at Truro.

Above: This letter, from a lucky passenger, thanks one of the rescuers for their help when the ship became stranded.

Right: It was decided to blow *Suevic*'s bow off and recover the aft section of the ship. Using dynamite, the bow was separated from the stern and the stern towed to Southampton for salvage.

Above left: One of the lifeboats of the *Suevic* at the Lizard.

Above right: A new bow was constructed at Belfast and still holds the distinction of being one of the few vessels in the world to be launched bow-ward. The new bow of *Suevic* is shown here sandwiched between two Royal Mail Steam Packet Co. ships at Southampton.

Right: RMS *Cretic* at Genoa, *c.*1905. She was built for F. Leyland at Hawthorn, Leslie on the Tyne in 1902 and launched as *Hanoverian*. In 1903 she was transferred to Dominion and renamed *Mayflower*, then transferred later that year to White Star. From 1904 she operated on the Boston-Mediterranean service. In 1923, she was transferred back to Leyland and broken up at Bo'ness in 1929.

Right: The *Suevic*'s new bow was towed across the Irish Sea from Belfast. It encountered a huge storm on the way but made it to Southampton safely.

Below right: Seen here soon after arrival at Southampton, the stern of *Suevic* awaits the new bow before the pair were mated together in dry dock..

In 1907, White Star transferred its express service from Liverpool to Southampton. The service was opened by the newly-built *Adriatic* on 5 June 1907. Starting from Southampton meant that the ships could call into a French port and collect immigrants from Europe, thus providing additional income for the ships. For the ever important mail contract, the mail could be in London faster than from Liverpool or Queenstown. Stops were made at Cherbourg outward and Plymouth inward and the mails were discharged at Plymouth for travel by rail to London.

With the purchase of White Star, there had been a fleet rationalization and White Star had been given the profitable Liverpool-Boston route as well as a Mediterranean service. Ships were transferred and Dominion Line had the Canadian routes. Atlantic Transport Line's *Minnewaska* became *Arabic* (II), the Dominion Line's *Commonwealth, New England, Columbus* and *Mayflower* became *Canopic, Romanic, Republic* (II) and *Cretic* respectively in 1903. From Leyland came four cargo vessels; *Victorian* and *Armenian* (transferred with the same names), and *American* and *European* (*Cufic* (II) and *Tropic* (II) respectively).

In 1905 *Germanic* left the fleet to become Dominion Line's *Ottawa*. She was to survive a further 45 years after being sold to Turkey. In the same year, White Star and Shaw Savill purchased 67 per cent of the management shares of Geo. Thompson's Aberdeen Line, further strengthening the two companies on the Antipodean run.

With the abandonment of *Olympic* in 1899, plans were made for a new ship – to be the largest vessel in the world, and the first to eclipse the *Great Eastern* of 1858 in every dimension. She was Harland & Wolff's keel No.315 and would be launched as *Celtic* on 4 April 1901. Painted in a light grey for her launch, mainly for the benefit of the many photographers, she was handed over to White Star in July 1901. The two men in the foreground are standing amidst hull plating for *Celtic*, the middle of the three ships under construction. `

Harland & Wolff's Shipbuilding Yard, Belfast.

Above: The next ship of what would become known as the 'Big Four' was *Cedric*. This view is of her promenade deck *c.*1906.

Below: The Launch! *Celtic* makes her first trip into her natural environment. The drag chains seen in the previous view would stop her in a few hundred feet and she was then marshalled by tugs into the fitting out area.

THE BIG FOUR

With the death of T.H. Ismay in 1899, and the cancellation of *Oceanic*'s sister ship, *Olympic* (I), Harland and Wolff set about designing a new ship for White Star. The vessel was to be the largest ship in the world – the first to exceed in size the *Great Eastern* of 1858 and she was to be a modern marvel fitted out with every conceivable luxury then available. Launched at Belfast on 4 April 1901, she went down the slipways painted all-over in grey so that she would photograph well for the press as she reached her natural environment for the first time. *Celtic* was not only important for her size, she was also built for comfort rather than speed and, although her design was capable of 19kt, her engines were economical and could push her at a service speed of only 16kt. At this speed she consumed 280 tons of coal per day making her very economical. Cargo capacity was huge at 17,000 tons in seven holds and it could take up to a week to turnaround at either New York or Liverpool.

On 11 July, she was handed over to White Star and left Liverpool on her maiden voyage on 26 July arriving on New York, where the channel had to be deepened for her, on 4 August. In 1902 she made a Mediterranean cruise from New York with 800 passengers and in 1904 she carried 2,957 passengers westbound – a company record.

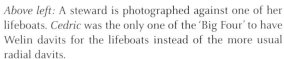

Above left: A steward is photographed against one of her lifeboats. *Cedric* was the only one of the 'Big Four' to have Welin davits for the lifeboats instead of the more usual radial davits.

Above right: Man Overboard! One does wonder what the attraction was.

Below right: A rather storm-battered *Cedric* in the Mersey, c.1920. In New York when *Titanic* sank, *Cedric* brought many of her crew back home to the UK. Her final voyage was in 1931 and she was sold for scrap, leaving Liverpool on 11 January 1932 for Inverkeithing and dismantling.

Above: Being towed by *Magnetic*, one of the 'Big Four' arrives at Liverpool's landing stage *c.*1910. The ships had huge cargo capacity and turnaround was a week at each port.

Above left: Baltic, the third of the four, at the landing stage in Liverpool. The ships burned about 300 tons of coal per day in comparison to the 1,000 tons plus of the four stacker Cunard flagships.

Left: With her captain looking on, *Adriatic* arrives at the White Star piers in New York in 1908. *Baltic* is already berthed there.

Below: Adriatic on her maiden arrival into Southampton to inaugurate the new White Star Line service from the port in June 1907.

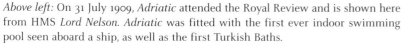

Above left: On 31 July 1909, *Adriatic* attended the Royal Review and is shown here from HMS *Lord Nelson*. *Adriatic* was fitted with the first ever indoor swimming pool seen aboard a ship, as well as the first Turkish Baths.

Above right: *Adriatic* at the Landing Stage, Liverpool, with *Magnetic* at her side.

Right: This view of the Mersey shows one of the 'Big Four', *c.*1906 and gives an idea of just how busy the port was. In fact, liners were only allowed to berth at the landing stage to embark and disembark passengers and all cargo was discharged at the company's berths in the dock system. It also shows one of the Isle of Man Steam Packet paddle steamers, numerous tenders, tugs and Mersey ferries as well as the two liners in view.

Above left: Unloading Swift's Beef from SS *Baltic* in the docks at Bootle. This Wright & Co. of Bootle postcard shows a traction engine as well as the ubiquitous horses and carts.

Above right: Celtic as an armed merchant cruiser during 1915. She was commissioned on 4 August 1914 and fitted with eight 6in guns. In January 1916 she was converted for trooping and in February 1917 hit a mine. She was repaired but in 1918 she was hit by a torpedo from UB-77. Again, she survived to fight another day.

Opposite *above left: Cedric* leaving Liverpool for the breaker's yard in Inverkeithing, Fife.

Opposite above right: Adriatic in the Mersey, being coaled, c. 1910. Is the small lighter steaming towards her *Pontic*, the company's water tender.

Opposite below left: A busy scene in the Gladstone Dock, Liverpool, in 1928.

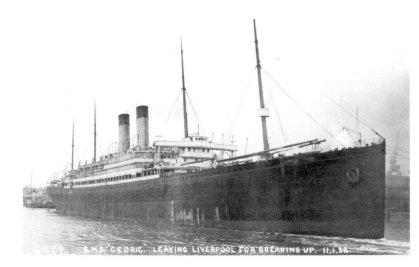

R.M.S. 'CEDRIC'. LEAVING LIVERPOOL FOR BREAKING UP. 11.1.32.

Celtic, however, wasn't a one off. Plans had been made to build a fleet of sister ships and the first, *Cedric*, was launched on 21 August 1902, entering service on 31 January 1903. *Baltic* (II) followed *Cedric* down the ways on 21 November 1903, with entry into service on 23 June 1904 and a maiden voyage from Liverpool to New York on 29 June. While *Cedric* had been a similar size to *Celtic*, *Baltic* was a good 20ft longer and was of 23,876grt. She retained the same engines, which meant that she was underpowered until they were modified. As a result, she was never as economical as the earlier pair.

Ordered in 1903, but not launched until 20 September 1906, the last of the quartet was *Adriatic*. She was briefly the largest ship in the world, but literally by only an hour or so as *Mauretania* was launched on the same day. She was of 24,541grt and was 729ft in length. In keeping with White Star's luxury over speed concept she was the first ship to have a swimming pool and a Turkish baths on board, luxuries that would soon become commonplace on newer liners.

Each ship had become more luxurious and with the introduction of *Adriatic*, White Star moved their express route from Liverpool to Southampton. She made her maiden voyage from Liverpool on 8 May and returned from New York to Southampton, arriving on 5 June. On this route she was partnered by *Majestic*, *Oceanic* and *Teutonic*. In 1911, with the arrival of *Olympic*, she returned to the Liverpool berth.

1909 saw *Baltic* involved in the rescue of the passengers and crew from *Republic*. Only an hour out of New York, she set off for where the *Republic* was sinking and rescued 1,260 survivors. Using her wireless once more, on 14 April 1912 she warned *Titanic* of ice that had slowed *Baltic* to a crawl. IT was a warning that was to be ignored with fatal consequences. *Cedric* was in New York when *Titanic* sank and her sailing was delayed so that survivors could return to Britain. Bruce Ismay himself returned on *Adriatic* after the US Senate Enquiry into the sinking.

On the commencement of war with Germany and the Austro-Hungarian Empire *Celtic* and *Cedric* were requisitioned as armed merchant cruisers and fitted with eight 6in guns. *Adriatic* and *Baltic* remained on the New York run but were used as troopships or operated under the Liner Requisition Scheme later in the war. *Celtic* was mined and torpedoed during the war, both times with small loss of life. On 29 January 1918, *Cedric* rammed Canadian Pacific's *Montreal* and sank her.

During the 1920s, the ships again sailed from Liverpool, and in 1926 *Adriatic* commenced winter cruising from New York. She was also the first ship to enter the newly-opened Gladstone dock system in Liverpool on 10 July 1927. In 1928, *Celtic* was wrecked at Roches Point, Queenstown, while picking up her pilot in gale force winds. Forced onto the rocks, her hull was punctured and she was declared a total loss. A bridge was built to shore and her cargo salvaged. She was broken up where she lay, with iron from the Guion Line's *Chicago* (wrecked at the same location in 1898) being found under her keel.

Above left and rigtht: The end for *Celtic.* She ran aground on 10 December 1928 at Roches Point, Queenstown, just after picking up the pilot for the port. This view was taken the morning after, as her funnels were cut down within a few days as they restricted the view of the lighthouse. She was declared a total loss and her cargo salvaged by building a bridge from ship to shore. Broken up where she lay, it was a blow to the cash-strapped White Star Line.

Right: Celtic in the Gladstone dock system in the mid-1920s

Opposite left: *Celtic* at the Landing Stage, Liverpool.

Opposite right: *Cedric* on the stocks immediately prior to launch at Harland & Wolff.

R.M.S. "BALTIC" LEAVING FOR JAPAN. S.518.

WHITE STAR LINE R.M.S. "CEDRIC" 1903
MODEL TO SCALE OF 1 INCH =100 FEET MADE BY LESLIE WILSON
WITH WOOD FROM A FITTING OUT OF THE "CEDRIC" VIZ. A
MIDSHIPS PORT PASSAGEWAY DOOR FOUND AT FELIN DRE
NEWMARKET, FLINTSHIRE 1939, "CEDRIC" HAVING BEEN
BROKEN UP IN 1932

With worsening trade conditions during the late 1920s, the remaining ships were occasionally laid up at Liverpool. On 5 September 1931, *Cedric* made her last voyage to New York and was sold for scrap soon afterwards, being replaced by the new motorship, *Britannic*. She was sold to Ward's at Inverkeithing for £22,150 and left Liverpool for the last time on 11 January 1932. On 17 September 1932, *Baltic* made her last voyage to New York and was replaced by *Georgic*, White Star's last new ship. On 1 October she was laid up at Liverpool and was sold to shipbreakers in Japan, leaving for Osaka on 17 February 1933. The largest and most modern of the ships, *Adriatic*, lasted longer, making her last voyage to New York on 24 February 1934. Unlike the other ships, this was not to be her last voyage as she was used for cruising throughout the year. In July 1934 she became the only one of the Big Four to join the new Cunard White Star combine but was declared redundant and put up for sale. *Adriatic* made her last cruise out of Liverpool in September 1934 and was sold in the November for £48,000. On 19 December she left Liverpool for Osaka, arriving there in March 1935. It was to be the end of White Star's most successful group of ships.

Above left: Baltic and *Adriatic* went slightly further than Scotland to be broken, both making the long journey to Osaka in Japan for final dismantling. Here *Baltic* leaves Liverpool on what was to be her final and longest voyage.

Left: A postcard view of a scale model made out of a door from *Cedric*.

Right: Photographed at Liverpool in July 1909, this view shows some of the officer cadets aboard the White Star Line's training ship *Mersey*. The SV *Mersey* was purchased by Bruce Ismay in 1908 for use as a sail training ship for eighty cadets.

Below left: *Mersey* was painted in an almost white livery for White Star and fitted with wireless in 1914. In 1915 she was put up for sale and sold to the Transatlantic Motorship Co. of Christiana, Norway, and renamed *Transatlantic*. Within a year she was sold again and renamed *Christian Radich*. In 1923 she was scrapped in the UK. This postcard was written from on board and carries the ship's extremely rare cachet stamp on the front.

Below right: Shown here in her original livery, she was one of five sisters for James Nourse and built in June 1894.

ownership, after which came near sisters *Baltic* (II) and *Adriatic* (II). These ships were built for comfort, not speed and each one was larger than the previous vessel, with each being the largest ship in the world at the time of launching. They were among the most up to date and technologically advanced liners but were also designed to carry large amounts of cargo (up to 17,000 tons). Their leisurely sailing schedule meant that there was plenty of time at either end of the voyage to load and unload cargo and the ships were immensely profitable as a result.

Three years later, White Star announced a £2.5M increase in capital, primarily to fund the construction of two or three new superliners at the Belfast yard of Harland & Wolff. The new ships would involve the rebuilding of the Belfast yard too, to accommodate the vessels, two of which were to be built side by side in a show of confidence in White Star. They were destined to become the most famous trio of ships ever constructed.

1909 was a bad year though, the company lost the *Republic* after she was rammed by the Italian Lloyd Italiano emigrant ship *Florida*. The loss of Republic, in fog, was a major blow, only mitigated by the fact that the sinking was the first time wireless had been used to save life at sea and that only four lost their lives as a result. Republic was reputedly carrying gold to help in the relief efforts in Messina, Sicily, after the earthquake that devastated the city. She has been dived on to this day, having sunk in only 34 fathoms, but little trace of the elusive gold has ever been found.

Two ships, being built for Dominion, were transferred to White Star and they inaugurated the White Star-Dominion Line Joint Service to Canada. The ships were *Megantic* and *Laurentic* (I). In much the same way as *Caronia* and *Carmania* had pioneered the technology to be used on *Mauretania* and *Lusitania*, *Megantic* and *Laurentic* pioneered the engine technology used on the new express ships under construction at Belfast for White Star.

R.M.S. ATHENIC.

ARRIVAL of the 'ATHENIC' to Wellington Harbour
FRIENDS AWAITING PASSENGERS TO LAND.   2000
"ZAK" PHOTO: 6.10.08.

Opposite above: Athenic survived two wars, conversion into a whale factory ship, capture by the Germans, a sinking and still managed a useful life of sixty years, twenty-six of them with White Star. Built for the Shaw, Savill joint route to New Zealand in 1902, she was the first of three similar vessels for the route and after her eventful life was sold for scrap in 1962.

Opposite below: On 6 October 1908, the quay at Wellington, New Zealand, was filled with friends and relatives awaiting apssengers on the *Athenic*.

Above: A stern view of *Corinthic*. In 1931, she was broken up at Wallsend on the Tyne by Hughes, Bolckow & Co.

Below: In November 1913, a huge dock strike at Wellington, New Zealand, saw *Athenic*, extreme left, and one of her sisters in the bay. The dock workers refused to load the ships with cargo and riots ensued in Wellington. *Athenic* was the first ship to leave harbour after the strike started.

Above left: Ionic at Wellington, New Zealand, *c.*1910. She made her maiden voyage to Auckland on 16 January 1903. Used as a troopship during the First World War she was nearly sunk by torpedo on New Year's Eve, 1915 in the Mediterranean.

Above right: In 1934, when the White Star service to Australia and New Zealand was sold to Shaw Savill, *Ionic* went with the route. In 1937 she was sold for scrap and sold to Japan for dismantling. This view shows her flying both the Shaw Savill and White Star flags.

Left: *Ionic* at Hobart in 1908 with the SS *Warrimoo* and the SS *Westralia* berthed in front of her.

Above left: In 1909, many of the passengers of the *Republic* were saved by the *Baltic's* crew after she was rammed by the Italian liner *Florida* on 23 January 1909. Here, *Florida* is shown in New York, complete with her stove-in bow. *Republic* was not so lucky, sinking in over 300ft of water, supposedly with a cargo of gold bullion.

Above right and right: The *Republic* in the Mersey c.1905. *Republic* was one of five ships transferred within IMMC to White Star and had originally been Dominion Line's *Columbus,* having served with Dominion for all of two months before being given to White Star in December 1903. She is famous as the ship where radio was first used to help rescue survivors after shipwreck. James Binns, her radio operator, used CQD, the then internationally recognised distress signal, to call for rescue.

Above: In 1908, with the launch of *Laurentic* on 9 September, White Star signalled its intention to enter the Canadian market. This had been the preserve of Dominion, and *Laurentic* had been laid down as *Alberta* for that line. She was the first White Star ship to be powered by reciprocating engines and a low pressure turbine powering the central propeller shaft, and can be considered as the test bed for the huge engines of *Olympic*, *Titanic* and *Britannic*.

Below: *Laurentic* at speed in a rather choppy Irish Sea. *Laurentic* was sunk on 25 January 1917, while carrying a £5M shipment of gold to Canada. Lost in 125ft of water off Lough Swilly with the loss of 354 lives, attempts were made to find her and the first diver was on the wreck on 9 February. Gales and the movement of the gold within the ship saw salvage abandoned but from 1919 to 1924 £4,958,000 of the gold was recovered. Twenty-five bars, then worth £41,292, still remain in and around the wreck today. The salvage cost only £128,000.

Right: A letter sent by a passenger on *Megantic* in August 1911, with the interesting comment that 'The manager of the line is on board, and has searched us out, and evidently we shall get special attention.'

Opposite above: HMS *Racer* leaving Portsmouth in March 1922 to salvage gold from the wreck of the *Laurentic*.

Opposite below: *Laurentic*'s sister was *Megantic*, but she was built with twin screws and quadruple expansion engines. The idea was that White Star could compare engines in two otherwise identical vessels. She was to have been named *Albany* for Dominion Line but was renamed before launching. This view shows her in the Mersey in 1909.

On board S.S. "MEGANTIC."

Aug 5 1911

"OLYMPIC" 45,000 TONS & "TITANIC" 45,000 TONS
LARGEST STEAMERS IN THE WORLD.
(BUILDING)

Dear Goosie.

Two letters in one day This boat is fine, new; & well equipped throughout. no motion or vibration noticable. Wouldn't hardly know you were moving – A pleasant company on board – 107 first class passengers, The food is excellent & abundant and in great variety. Shall have to look that I do not gain – The manager of line is on board, and has searched us out, and evidently we shall get special attention

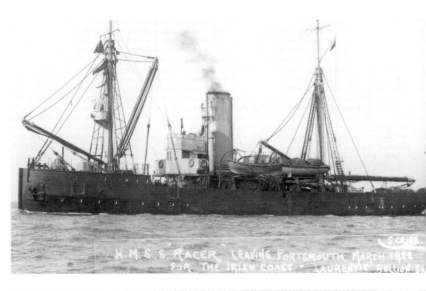

H.M.S.S. "RACER" LEAVING PORTSMOUTH MARCH 1922 FOR THE IRISH COAST - LAURENTIC BULLION SA

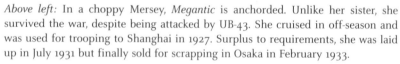

Above left: In a choppy Mersey, *Megantic* is anchorded. Unlike her sister, she survived the war, despite being attacked by UB-43. She cruised in off-season and was used for trooping to Shanghai in 1927. Surplus to requirements, she was laid up in July 1931 but finally sold for scrapping in Osaka in February 1933.

Above right: *Megantic* at Liverpool sometime in the 1920s.

Right: *Zealandic*, another ship built for the New Zealand route, held the record for the largest cargo of wool exported from New Zealand. Built in 1911, she was transferred to the Aberdeen Line in 1926 and renamed *Mamilius*. She then passed to Shaw Savill and was sold to the Admiralty in 1939. Like *Cevic* in the First War, she was converted into a dummy battleship, this time HMS *Hermes*, the aircraft carrier. After the real *Hermes* had been sunk she was wrecked off Cromer, Norfolk on 4 June 1941 and then sunk by an E-boat torpedo.

Chapter 4

FROM THE BIG THREE TO THE END OF THE WAR

On the day she was launched, *Baltic* lost her record as the largest ship in the world. Within a few hours the new Cunard express liner *Mauretania* entered the water and exceeded *Baltic's* total by some 7,000 tons. It was a blow to White Star's prestige, but planning of a new trio of ships had already begun and, in talks with Harland & Wolff, a plan was put in place to build new ships that would eclipse all on the North Atlantic. The planning had begun with the reconstruction of the Harland & Wolff Yard, As ships were launched from the Queens Island yard, men hurriedly began to clear the ways for a new series of slipways and a huge steel gantry that would tower over any ship being constructed in this part of the yard. The contract for the 'great gantry', as it became known, was awarded to Sir William Arrol's firm, the same company that had constructed the Forth Railway Bridge. Beneath its mighty span, two slipways were constructed, each large enough to accommodate the largest ship in the world, with space left over for future engineering triumphs. Also being built at Belfast at the same time was the Thompson Dry Dock, again large enough to take the new superliners.

The keel of the first of the new ships, simply known by her keel number, 400, was laid on 16 December 1908, while the next berth, No.3,

was still being prepared for her sister, No.401. Work continued apace, and on 20 October 1910, with little ceremony, the hull of the *Olympic*, as No.400 had become known, entered the water.

By 31 May 1911, her sister had reached the point when she too would enter her natural element for the first time. In a double ceremony, one ship was handed over while the other was launched, giving Belfast the accolade of most tonnage in a single port at the same time. Easily the largest ships in the world, both *Olympic* and her new sister, *Titanic*, were of 45,000grt, a full third larger than the *Lusitania* or *Mauretania*. Never designed to be the fastest, they would comfortably sail at 20kt all day long and, considering the size of their reciprocating steam engines, with a reasonable fuel consumption. With the advent of a third sister, they would operate a regular weekly service from Southampton to New York, or so it was planned. Olympic was rammed by HMS *Hawke* on 21 September 1911, causing damage severe enough to send her back to Harland & Wolff for repair. The loss of a propeller blade the following February delayed the maiden voyage of her almost-completed sister, *Titanic*.

A huge chunk of ice in the mid-Atlantic put paid to White Star's plans. With the third sister, *Gigantic*, already planned to be larger than *Titanic*, an iceberg, a thousand lifetimes in the making, lay directly in *Titanic's* path. On the night of 14/15 April 1912, *Titanic* sank, taking over 1,500 people to their deaths and the dreams of a three ship express service with them.

Shortly after the *Titanic* sank, *Olympic* returned to Southampton. Her crew decided they would not sail on her until more lifeboats were added and mutiny ensued off Ryde. Within six months she would be back in Belfast for a major overhaul that saw not only a double hull fitted, but also two oil-fired boilers as a test of the new technology.

In order to maintain a regular sailing schedule after the sinking of *Titanic*, it was decided to reintroduce *Majestic* (I), which was laid up as reserve ship until *Titanic* sank, until the newest White Star superliner, now renamed *Britannic* (II), was ready.

While the Atlantic was receiving these huge ships, the routes to Australia were not forgotten and *Ceramic* entered service in 1913 as the largest ship to sail to Australia. She still holds the record for the tallest masts to go under the Sydney Harbour Bridge and wasn't equaled on the Australian route until P&O's *Mooltan* of 1923.

Launched in February 1914, the outbreak of the First World War brought the construction of *Britannic* to a halt, materials and labour being diverted from non-essential civil projects to the demands of the military instead.

Oceanic was wrecked off the coast of the Shetlands in September 1914 while operating as an armed merchant cruiserwhile, in 1915 the *Arabic* (II) was lost as was the *Armenian*. Both were sunk by U-Boats.

Britannic was hurriedly complete at Harland & Wolff as a hospital ship. The opening of the Gallipoli campaign had given the British superliners a new use – as troop transports and hospital ships. On 21 November

In 1908, after *Laurentic* was launched, a rebuilding took place in the yard at Harland & Wolff's and three slips were rebuilt into two in preparation for the construction of the world's largest ships. A huge new gantry was built by Sir William Arrol, and it would dominate the Belfast skyline until demolition and replacement by two other Belfast landmarks – *Samson* and *Goliath*. Shown here in early 1909 are the keels of Hull Nos 400 and 401, destined to become the most famous sister ships ever built.

Above: This view of *Olympic* gives an idea of the sheer scale of the great gantry, which towered over even the largest ships in the world. *Titanic* sits behind her with work continuing apace on her too.

Left: 'All steamers built in Ireland', proclaimed this poster, designed by Montague B. Black and destined for the local emigrant market, for *Olympic* (Hull 400) and *Titanic* (Hull 401). Interestingly, little is known about Black and it is a mystery as to when and where he died. He was one of the finest of the marine artists of the twentieth century.

The World's Greatest Gantry, in Harland & Wolff's North Shipyard, Belfast.

Above: Olympic and *Titanic* together – with *Olympic* almost ready for launching. *Titanic* is still having her hull plated.

Right: Like *Celtic*, over a decade before, *Olympic* was painted in light grey to aid the photographers as she was launched. This time, however, a new graving dock had been built in Belfast and she went down the ways without propellers fitted.

Above left: It took 62s for *Olympic* to enter the water on 20 October 1910.

Above right: As *Olympic* was the largest ship in the world by a large margin, White Star used this type of comparison to get the message across to potential customers.

Below left: Olympic at Belfast, with *Mammoth*, Harland & Wolff's floating crane behind. This view, on a postcard by local postcard publisher Hurst, shows the new Thompson Dry Dock.

Below right: Olympic left Belfast on 31 May 1911 and headed for Liverpool, where she was open to the public for the day. Here she is, anchored in the Mersey.

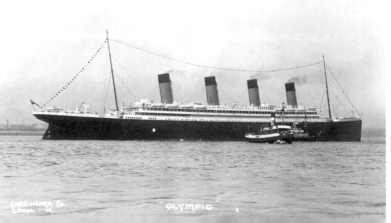

Above: Olympic off Cowes on 20 September 1911, with a Red Funnel paddle steamer about to sail past. Her starboard side had been holed by HMS *Hawke*.

Left and below: On 20 September 1911, outward bound from Southampton, *Olympic*, under the command of Captain E.J. Smith, was rammed by the cruiser HMS *Hawke*, causing a huge gash on the stern of *Olympic* and the bows to be stove in on *Hawke*. The damage put *Olympic* out of commission for six weeks.

S.S. "OLYMPIC" DISCHARGING OCEAN MAILS AT PLYMOUTH.

Above left: An original 1912 watercolour of *Olympic* discharging mails at Plymouth.

Above right: An original 1912 advertising postcard for RMS *Olympic*.

Right: Olympic and *Titanic* were to meet one last time, in February 1912. *Olympic* had to return to Belfast for repairs, which led to the delay in *Titanic's* maiden voyage.

Above left: Olympic's second-class promenade deck

Above right: The Grand Staircase showing the clock 'Honour & Glory over Time'. Parts of this staircase survive in the White Swan Hotel, Alnwick, and the clock survives in Southampton.

Below left: The first-class restaurant.

1916, never having carried a fare-paying passenger and never having sailed across the Atlantic, *Britannic* (II) was sunk off Mudros by a mine. Thankfully, she was almost empty, being on the outward voyage but, nonetheless, thirty-four people still died when she sank in 400ft of water. She remains to this day well preserved and as the largest shipwreck of both world wars. Her massive engines, the largest reciprocating steam engines ever made, lie in the submerged hulk.

Above left: Olympic's first-class reception room.

Above right: Olympic was only the second ocean liner to have an indoor swimming pool.

Below right: The garden lounge aboard *Olympic*

Above left: A first-class bedroom on board *Olympic*.

Above right: The sitting room of a first-class suite.

Left: Olympic's captain was E.J. Smith, who had been with the company for many years. He was supposedly to retire in 1912 after taking the Titanic on her maiden voyage. .

Below: Titanic, built at *Olympic*'s side, was ever so slightly larger, because of her enclosed promenade deck. Here she is shown in Belfast Lough on her maiden voyage to Southampton in April 1912.

Above left: Montague Black's rendition of an *Olympic*-class liner at sea was an instant classic and was used in much company-generated publicity.

Middle: The White Star Line offices at James Street, Liverpool, looked down onto the company's berth at the landing stage.

Above right: Because of delays caused in her construction, *Titanic* was sailed directly to Southampton and never ever visited her home port of Liverpool. This view shows her on Good Friday, 1912, when she was opened briefly to the paying public. There had been a coal strike on and coal for her voyage was scavenged from other IMM vessels in port. A barge-full can be seen at her bow.

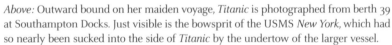

Above: Outward bound on her maiden voyage, *Titanic* is photographed from berth 39 at Southampton Docks. Just visible is the bowsprit of the USMS *New York*, which had so nearly been sucked into the side of *Titanic* by the undertow of the larger vessel.

Above right: Titanic being coaled prior to her maiden voyage of 10 April 1912.

Below right: Titanic pulls away from Berth 43 at the Ocean Dock, Southampton, on her first and last voyage. First Officer Murdoch and a quartermaster are on the aft docking bridge.

Opposite page: Sent by a Second Class passenger, this postcard was posted from *Titanic* when she stopped at Queenstown. Jack, however, did not survive.

WHITE STAR LINE.

THE LARGEST STEAMERS IN THE WORLD.

THE LARGEST STEAMERS IN THE WORLD.

"OLYMPIC" (TRIPLE-SCREW), 45,000 TONS,
AND
"TITANIC" (TRIPLE-SCREW), 45,000 TONS.

POST CARD.

W. H. Stone
Tregoniserey
St Austell
Cornwall
England

Dear Bill just a
line to you old boy
just to let you
know I am alright
and well and I
hope you are the
same you can
remember me to
all well good
bye from Jack

Above left: Photographed from Ryde by W.R. Hogg, *Titanic* is passing the warships seen in the circular view on the previous page.

Above right: The only known photograph of the radio room of the SS *Californian*, of the Leyland Line, this view was taken in May 1914 and shows Murphy at the key.

Opposite page, clockwise from top left: *Titanic* steamed into an iceberg, but the ice field it contained covered hundreds of square miles. Passengers view the ice from an unknown ship.

The iceberg, seen from on board *Carpathia*.

Just after 8.00 a.m. *Titanic*'s last lifeboat was recovered. These boats could carry upwards of seventy people, yet this one is not even half full.

One of the few full lifeboats at *Carpathia*'s side. Most of the lifeboats were recovered and taken back to New York.

ITANIC" LIFEBOAT ALONGSIDE "CARPATHIA"

Memorial Service

Held in

Brunswick St. Methodist Ch.

HALIFAX

Friday, May 3rd, 11 a. m.

On the occasion of the Burial of many Bodies recovered from the Sea after the Titanic Disaster.

Opening Sentences and Invocation ....
Rev G W F Glendenning

Hymn—"Forever with the Lord"
Accompanied by the Band of the R C R

"Forever with the Lord!"
Amen! so let it be!
Life from the dead is in that word,
'Tis immortality!
Here in the body pent,
Absent from him I roam,
Yet nightly pitch my moving tent
A day's march nearer home.

Above left: On 27 April, *Olympic* started on her next voyage to the USA, but portions of the crew mutinied and she was laid up at Ryde until the strike over safety and the poor quality of the new lifeboats was resolved. Another W.R. Hogg view.

Above right: The lifeboats in the foreground were fitted to *Olympic* upon her arrival in Southampton from New York. They had come from the laid-up P&O troopship on the right in this view of the Ocean Dock.

Left: Meanwhile, the *Mackay Bennett* and *Minea* had been sent out from Halifax to search for bodies and recover as many as possible. The identified (or obviously first-class) passengers' bodies were recovered while the unidentified bodies were buried at sea.

Above left: Olympic opened for public inspection after her 1912/13 refit. During this refit she was fitted, according to *Railway & Travel Monthly*, with two oil-fired boilers as an experiment. This experiment must have been successful as she was fitted for oil burning immediately after the end of the First World War, the first White Star ship to be so converted.

Above right: It had always been planned to build a third sister and her name, *Gigantic,* was changed subtly after the *Titanic* disaster to *Britannic*. As a result of the disaster, *Britannic* was totally redesigned and had a new double hull constructed. This view shows her keel with the stern plate fitted, with the keel of the Holland America Line's *Statendam* behind. The war would overtake events and *Statendam* finally sailed as *Justicia* for White Star.

WHITE STAR LINE R.M.S. "BRITANNIC" 50,000 TONS.
LAUNCHED FEB. 26TH 1914

CHERBOURG - Le " TRAFFIC " bateau transbordeur de la " White star Line "
quitte la gare Maritime

Edition Verschuere

Above left: Built at the same time as *Olympic* were the tenders *Nomadic* and *Traffic*, both for use at Cherbourg, where the ships anchored in the outer harbour and passengers and luggage were brought out to them. *Nomadic* was the first-class tender and *Traffic*, shown here, was the baggage tender and also carried third-class passengers.

Above right: While *Britannic* was under construction, another new vessel entered service. *Ceramic* was built for the Australian route and was the largest vessel serving it on her entry into service in 1912. On 23 November 1942 she left Liverpool bound for South Africa but was sunk on the evening of 6/7 December. All but one of the 656 people on board were lost. The sole survivor was lucky enough to be picked up by a U-boat and spent the rest of the war as a prisoner of war.

Opposite left: Her frames are in place and the huge stocks of steel in the foreground are for plating the hull. In the previous view, workmen can be seen with a huge riveting machine, plating the deck.

Opposite right: A company-issued postcard of *Britannic*, in a livery she was never to carry. She was fitted with large davits capable of handling many boats and it was originally intended that she should carry six davits, but was built with fewer.

Opposite below: Looking down from the great gantry onto what would become the bridge front of *Britannic*.

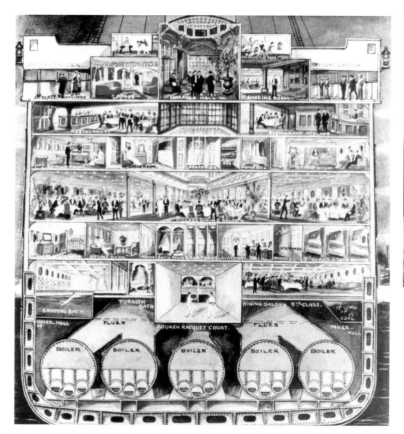

Above left: A cutaway of *Britannic*, showing her double skin.

Above right: A unique view of *Britannic*, two days before her launch, with the steam pile-driver removing the caission wall at the end of her slipway.

Right: On 22 April 1914 the *Titanic* Memorial was unveiled in Southampton.

The Sinking of H.M.S. "Audacious" in the Irish Sea, by a German Mine, during the Great War 1914.

Abrahams & Sons
Devonport.

As the stern of HMS *Audacious*, the Birkenhead-built Dreadnought battleship, starts to slip below the waves, the lifeboats of RMS *Olympic* rescue the crew from the stricken vessel.

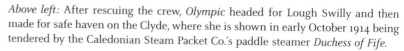

Above left: After rescuing the crew, *Olympic* headed for Lough Swilly and then made for safe haven on the Clyde, where she is shown in early October 1914 being tendered by the Caledonian Steam Packet Co.'s paddle steamer *Duchess of Fife*.

Above right: Olympic on 18 August 1918, from 800 feet.

Left: Olympic trooping at Mudros in 1915. Although the big liners had been rejected as armed merchant cruisers because of their astronomical fuel consumption, the start of the Gallipoli campaign required huge numbers of troops and wounded to be moved quickly. Here ships like *Mauretania*, *Britannic*, *Aquitania* and *Olympic* came into their own. At least one gun can clearly be seen on *Olympic*'s bow.

Opposite: Later in the war, *Olympic* was used to bring troops from Canada. Here she is being coaled at Halifax, Nova Scotia, having embarked another three thousand or so for France.

S.S. OLYMPIC.

Above left: Olympic being coaled in the Firth of Clyde in 1916, as photographed from HMS *Patia*.

Above right: In October 1914 a convoy left Gaspe Bay, Canada, with thirty-two troopships and an escort of five warships. It was the single largest movement of men and equipment at the time. Both *Megantic* and *Laurentic* took part and arrived at Plymouth on 14 October. They are shown here side by side and with the Royal Mail Steam Packet Co.'s RMS *Bermudian*.

Left: Shown at Belfast is HMS *Queen Mary*, just about to be decommissioned in 1915. Well, actually, it was White Star's *Cevic*, converted to look like the battleship in 1914 and shown here about to be re-converted back into a cargo ship.

TWIN SCREW STEAMER "ZEELAND."

2ND. CLASS.

September 15th, 19[1]

DINNER.

Clam Chowder

Hake—Anchovy Sauce

Sea Pie

Roast Lamb—Mint Sauce

Boiled Fowl—Creamed Macaroni

Mashed Carrots & Turnips   Boiled Rice

Browned and Boiled Potatoes

Chancellor Pudding   Jam Tartlets

Ice Cream

Above left: As well as dummy battleships, some White Star vessels became real battleships. Converted into an armed merchant cruiser, *Teutonic* is shown leaving the Mersey in battleship grey with 6in guns fore and aft. This view dates from 1915, by which time *Teutonic* had been purchased by the Admiralty.

Above right: Northland was renamed from *Zeeland*, as the original name was consider too Germanic. In 1915 she was converted for trooping. She had been built for Red Star originally and spent much of her life in their service as well as with White Star. Broken up at Inverkeithing in 1930, she had led an interesting life for Red Star, White Star and as *Minnesota* for the Atlantic Transport Line.

Right: A menu for the *Zeeland* from 1911, two days after she had been transferred by White Star to the Red Star Line.

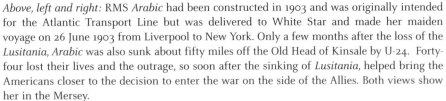

Above, left and right: RMS *Arabic* had been constructed in 1903 and was originally intended for the Atlantic Transport Line but was delivered to White Star and made her maiden voyage on 26 June 1903 from Liverpool to New York. Only a few months after the loss of the *Lusitania*, *Arabic* was also sunk about fifty miles off the Old Head of Kinsale by U-24. Forty-four lost their lives and the outrage, so soon after the sinking of *Lusitania*, helped bring the Americans closer to the decision to enter the war on the side of the Allies. Both views show her in the Mersey.

Right: HMNZT *Athenic* at Wellington, New Zealand. Shown here about to make another trooping voyage to Britain is the New Zealand Transport No.11. As well as troops and equipment, *Athenic* still carried much-needed meat in her refrigerated and frozen holds.

KEEP THIS CARD   40

Your Quarters are on
DECK   D

COMPARTMENT A 2 Aft.

You will occupy
ONE HAMMOCK   A 2
You will Mess in COMPARTMENT

At Mess No. | 5 | FIRST SITTING
| | SECOND SITTING

Above: Britannic, laid up, half completed at Belfast, was hurriedly converted into a hospital ship when the scale of the military disaster in the Dardanelles was becoming obvious. On 8 December 1915, she was handed over as a hospital ship for 3,300 patients and made a maiden voyage from Belfast to Alexandria. She then headed for Mudros, where she is shown here, with HMS *Triad* and HMS *Nelson*.

Top right: Towards the end of the war, *Olympic* spent much time trooping from Canada. This berthing card belonged to a Canadian soldier aboard one of her 1917 voyages.

Opposite: Shown here in a classic pose, *Olympic* is painted in her dazzle paint livery with 6in guns fore and aft on a trooping voyage from Canada on 3 September 1918, photographed from 1,000ft.

Right: Perhaps one of the best ever images of *Britannic,* shown here being coaled at Southampton in early 1916. She carries the number G.608 on her bridge.

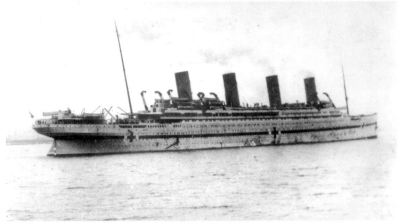

Above left: With the sinking of *Britannic*, White Star had a crew without a ship. Cunard had been promised the ex-*Statendam*, which was still under construction at Belfast, but the crew of *Lusitania* had been dispersed. It was decided that the crew of *Britannic* should be used to man the *Justicia*, as *Statendam* had become. Here she is, photographed from the Elders & Fyffe's banana boat and now armed-merchant-cruiser, HMS *Patia*, outward bound from New York on 19 May 1918.

Above right: Outward bound from Southampton in 1916, *Britannic* leaves for another voyage to Mudros. When she arrived back, a whole fleet of special hospital trains would be waiting to remove the injured to hospitals throughout the UK. Many of the seriously injured would end up in the hospital at Netley, and there was even a special hospital ship that sailed from Southampton to Netley, carrying the injured.

Left: On 19 July 1918, on the return to New York from Belfast, *Justicia* was torpedoed by UB-64. Despite concerted efforts by the escorting destroyers, three more torpedoes struck from UB-64. Next day UB-124 fired two torpedoes into the side of *Justicia*. They were to prove fatal and she sank lower and lower in the water until she slipped below the waves at noon.

Gallic in the Mersey. *Gallic* was one of a series of twenty-two ships built to a standard design by the Shipping Controller. White Star managed the vessel and in 1919 purchased it and renamed it *Gallic* for the Australian cargo service.

HMT ZEPPELIN LEAVING SOUTHAMPTON

Above left: HMT *Zeppelin* was acquired from North German Lloyd, who handed the ship over to Britain as war reparation. For a year the vessel was used as a troopship and managed by White Star, before being sold to the Orient Line and renamed *Ormuz*.

Above right: *Bardic* with a salvage ship at her side, and the pumps working overtime, at the Lizard.

Left: *Delphic* was purchased in 1925.

Later that that same year, the *Georgic* was captured and sunk off Cape Race by the German raider *Moewe* and four days later the *Russian* was torpedoed near Malta. With £5M of gold bullion on board, the sinking of *Laurentic* off Ireland in January 1917 was a major blow not only to White Star but also the British Government. 1917 was mostly a good year though as White Star inherited two ships that had been building at Belfast before the war started: *Belgic* (IV) was to have been the Red Star's *Belgenland* and *Justicia*, which was being built as Holland America's *Statendam*. *Justicia* had obviously been intended for Cunard to replace the *Lusitania* but White Star had the crew of *Britannic* ready to man the new vessel. *Delphic* and *Southland* were both lost to the enemy in 1917.

Justicia, suffered at the hands of a German submarine, being sunk in July 1918, having served for White Star for fourteen months only. At the war's end the tally of ships sunk included *Oceanic, Armenian, Arabic, Britannic, Georgic, Russian, Laurentic, Afric, Southland, Delphic* and *Justicia*. The biggest loss was *Olympic*'s running mate, *Britannic* and it was a loss that was to have a huge impact post-war.

Above left: Bardic was purchased by White Star in 1919 and was sold out of service in 1925 after she had come ashore on the Stag Rock. This view shows water being pumped out as she sits high and dry, with a salvage vessel behind her.

Below left: Vedic was launched by Harland & Wolff in 1917, although the design had been planned in 1913. In 1918 she made White Star's first sailing from Glasgow to Boston and was used on a variety of the company's routes. In 1934, declared surplus, she was sold for £10,400 and scrapped at Rosyth.

Above left: The Lizard lifeboat is launched to the *Bardic's* rescue on 31 August 1924.

Above right: Another view of *Bardic*, showing some of her cargo being unloaded in an effort to refloat her. She was eventually transferred to the Aberdeen Line and then to Shaw Savill. In 1941 she was sunk by the pocket battleship *Scharnhorst* while near the Cape Verde islands.

Chapter 5

THE LAST OF THE LINE

After the war, life began to return to normal. White Star initiated a rebuilding programme to replace the ships which had been lost in the war. Under war reparation, White Star also received ships from Germany to replace ships lost during the war. The former Norddeutscher Lloyd liner *Berlin* was given to White Star and Hamburg America Line's *Bismarck* was purchased where she lay to become *Majestic* (II). She recaptured for White Star, the honour of biggest ship in the world, although it was 1922 before the ship entered service as she needed extensive finishing work to complete her. NDL's *Columbus* was also acquired as a running mate for *Olympic* and *Majestic* on the express run from Southampton but never proved a match for the other two vessels.

White Star Line purchased the *Gallic* (II) and *Bardic* from the British government's Shipping Controller. While *Bardic* was used for the Liverpool to New York service, *Gallic* (II) was put on the Australian route to become a cargo carrier. Their sister ship, *Delphic* (II) joined the fleet in 1925 after a period as *Mesaba* for the Atlantic Transport Line. This replaced *Bardic* which, soon after her grounding off Land's End, was sold to the Aberdeen Line. In 1925, White Star gave the required notice to

Harland & Wolff that it would stop the 'cost plus' system of ordering ships and require the company to tender for them at a fixed price.

With the resurgence of the German shipping lines, in 1926, White Star Line stopped its German emigrant services from Hamburg. The joint White Star-Dominion service to Canada also ceased in 1925 with the selling for scrap of Dominion's RMS *Canada*, leaving White Star to operate the service alone.

By November 1926, White Star had become a British-owned company again. The war had created huge problems for the IMM, what with the loss of so many ships, total lack of investment and the death of J.P. Morgan himself in March 1913. When Morgan died, the other directors of the company were less enthusiastic about the sums of money required to create a monopoly and only the advent of war kept IMM together for so long. IMM let it be known that White Star was for sale and the Furness Withy group tried to buy the company for £3.5M. The General Strike in Britain put paid to the negotiations and a few months later it was announced that Lord Kyslant's Royal Mail Lines had purchased White Star. Almost the first act of Royal Mail was to send a letter to Harland &

Wolff cancelling the new tender terms for shipbuilding. It was hardly a coincidence that Kylsant had owned Harland & Wolff since 1924, when Lord Pirrie died. It had cost £7.9M, including interest, to buy White Star, and Royal Mail had problems coming up with all the cash. The Royal Mail transferred the two ships it had on the New York run and *Ohio* and *Orca* became *Albertic* and *Calgaric*. It was an effective way of withdrawing some capital from White Star and would be the start of financial irregularities that would see the downfall of Kyslant. Both ships were placed on the Canadian service.

Kylsant had had a policy of building new ships and expanding during downturns in the industry, a policy made easier when you owned your own shipyard. This meant that he would be able to buy new tonnage at cheap prices. Unfortunately for him, this policy backfired as the world entered the Depression years. His reckless expansion had led to the Royal Mail group of companies running out of money at just the time that huge loans were due to be paid back to the Treasury.

In 1927, the one and only fixed-price ship was delivered to White Star. She was *Laurentic* (II), the last coal-fired Atlantic passenger ship

The Great Depression affected White Star Line's shipbuilding programme too. The contract for the replacement of *Homeric*, the motorship *Oceanic*, was cancelled soon after the keel had been laid. The ship was to have been the world's largest motorship, at over 60,000grt and 1,010ft in length, and would have cost £3.5M. In 1928, *Athenic*, *Medic* and *Suevic* were all sold to become whaling factory ships while *Celtic* went aground on 10 December at Roches Point, Queenstown, and was declared a total loss. Kylsant was also using the company as a vehicle to further his expansion, despite the fact that his companies could ill-afford the money. White Star was used to purchase the remainder of the shares that Kylsant did not already own in Shaw, Savill & Albion and purchased the Australian Government's Aberdeen Line too.

Runic (II) was sold to the New Sevilla whaling company in 1930 while *Corinthic*, *Arabic* (III), *Cedric* and *Cufic* (II), *Baltic* (II), *Megantic*, *Tropic* (II) and *Albertic* were all sold to the breakers and were scrapped. *Gallic* (II) and *Delphic* (II) were sold to the Clan line for further trading. The only new builds to compensate for the shrinking of the fleet were White Star's only motorships, *Britannic* (III) and *Georgic* (II), both of about 27,000grt. Some of the steel used in *Britannic* was originally intended for *Oceanic*. The two ships were built as cabin-class liners.

In 1931, the end came for Royal Mail group and, as the company, slid irrevocably into bankruptcy, its chairman headed to jail. The banks agreed to let each line continue to operate until it could be sold to pay creditors. White Star, with its aging fleet of ships, many in dire need of replacement, was on a downward spiral that looked like it would only end in insolvency.

White Star was showing signs of severe financial strain. The British Government was watching with unease as it looked as if their troop-carrying capacity would be further depleted if White Star Line was sold again to foreign interests. After four years of losses, it looked likely that White Star would go bust. The company's main rival, Cunard, was also in severe difficulties and the government could not afford to bail both out. Something had to give and it was either the loss of one prestigious line or the merger of the two. After the intervention of the Government, the Cunard Line acquired 62 per cent of the shares in the new Cunard-White Star Line Ltd, with a new company, the Oceanic Steam Navigation Realisation Co. which held the remainder. The International Mercantile Marine became one of the new company's creditors, not having been paid in full by Royal Mail all those years ago.

The new Cunard-White Star company was given the go-ahead to complete the hull of No.534, languishing incomplete at Clydebank and a new liner of a similar size that would once and for all give a British company a weekly service to the United States. These liners were to become the *Queen Mary* and the *Queen Elizabeth*.

Meanwhile, *Homeric*, *Majestic* (II) and *Olympic* (II) remained on the Southampton to New York service, and *Britannic* (III) and *Georgic* (II) were on the Liverpool to New York route. On the Canadian route, only *Laurentic* (II) and *Doric* (II) remained. With a dominance in the new company and a more modern fleet, it was obvious that, in the current climate, Cunard ships would remain in service while the company rationalised its fleet.

During the fitting out of Cunard-White Star's new liner *Queen Mary*, the Old Reliable *Olympic* (II) was scrapped. Then a run of scrappings occurred as the remaining White Star Line ships were released from the fleet – *Majestic* (II) was sold for scrap but then purchased by the Admiralty to become the training ship HMS *Caledonia* at Rosyth, *Homeric*, always a weak ship even under White Star, was scrapped at Inverkeithing. *Calgaric*, unfortunately not required by the combine, was stripped at Rosyth and then broken up at Inverkeithing. *Laurentic* was used for cruising through the 1930s but in July 1935 was rammed by the Blue Star Line's *Napier Star*. Only her newness saved her from the scrapyard. The same could not be said for *Doric*. Rammed by the Chargeur Reunis liner *Formigny* barely a month later, she was deemed uneconomic to repair and headed under her own steam to Newport, Wales, for breaking. She was only twelve-years-old and was the largest ship to sail up the Usk at the time. *Laurentic* spent much of the next two years laid up, but was converted to an armed merchant cruiser at the beginning of the Second World War.

The war brought further misfortunes for the three remaining White Star Line ships. *Britannic* (III) and *Georgic* (II) were both used as troopships, with *Britannic* carrying 180,000 troops and sailing over 376,000 miles by the war's end. *Georgic* (II) was bombed at Port Tewfik, Egypt, and

extensively damaged, but after being taken to Bombay then Belfast, she was repaired and totally overhauled, leaving Belfast in December 1944 with a single funnel. *Laurentic* (II) was sunk by a torpedo from Otto Kretschmer's U-99 on 3 November 1940 with the loss of 49 lives.

After the end of the war, Cunard purchased the remaining 38 per cent of shares in Cunard-White Star Ltd. By 1949, Cunard then took over all of the company and the White Star name finally disappeared, although both *Georgic* and *Britannic* still flew White Star burgees and still carried buff funnels with black tops.

In 1947 *Britannic* reverted back to her owners and, after a major refit, was returned to service on the Liverpool-Cobh-New York run on 22 May 1948, with winter cruising out of New York. *Georgic*, after her near loss, was sold by Cunard-White Star to the Ministry of War Transport, although still managed by Cunard-White Star. She returned to service much later, being used to transport emigrants to Australia and New Zealand. In 1950 she was chartered back to Cunard and used on the New York service from Liverpool. On 19 October 1954, *Georgic* made her last sailing for the company, then performed some trooping voyages before being laid up at Kames Bay, Isle of Bute in 1955. Sold to Shipbreaking Industries, she made the short voyage to Faslane on 1 February 1956 for breaking at the same *site* as Cunard's *Aquitania*.

On 25 November 1960, making her 275th voyage, *Britannic* left New York bound for Liverpool. Engine problems had deemed her fit for the breaker's yard too. Arriving at Liverpool, she held the distinction of being White Star's last ocean-going passenger ship. On 4 December 1960 she was sold to British Iron & Steel Co. (Salvage) Ltd and, twelve days later, left Liverpool for the last time, this time empty of passengers and with only a skeleton crew. She sailed out of the Mersey and headed round the coast of Britain to the Firth of Forth, last resting place for so many famous Cunard and White Star liners from *Campania* to *Mauretania* (I), from

Majestic (II) to *Olympic* (II). Here she was broken up at the Thos W. Ward yard at Inverkeithing in 1961. Thus ended the story of one of the greatest and most well-known shipping lines in the world. Or was it?

Recently, Cunard has resurrected the White Star name to reflect its superior levels of service and attention to detail, and they have also named their Training Academy after the line.

One ship of the line still remains to this day, *Titanic's* first-class passenger tender, built in the Harland & Wolff yard at the same time as the ship she was meant to serve, has miraculously survived the best part of a century. When *Titanic* and *Olympic* were built, they were simply too large to enter the harbour at Cherbourg, choosing instead to anchor in the outer harbour, where they could be tendered by the company's smallest passenger ships. Built specially for the purpose were two tenders, *Traffic* and *Nomadic*. *Traffic*, designed to be used at any of the company's ports, was 675grt while *Nomadic* was 1,273grt. They tendered for *Olympic* at Belfast on her sea trials and then headed south, *Nomadic* for Southampton with *Olympic*, and *Traffic* for Cherbourg. Soon *Nomadic* was in Cherbourg too and she replaced the paddle tender *Gallic*. After being sold out of service, she ended up on England's South Coast during the Second World War. Escaping the fate of *Traffic*, sunk in the Channel in 1941, she returned to Cherbourg and survived until 1968 at the port. She was then sold for scrap, a fate she avoided, when she was purchased for use as a floating restaurant in Paris, next to the Eiffel Tower. Her future looked rather gloomy though when she was once again pensioned off. Languishing at Le Havre for a while, her superstructure cut down so she could travel down the Seine, she has recently been purchased and was safely delivered to her home city in July 2006. She is to feature as part of the *Titanic* Quarter, the sole remaining ship of the line. A five-year restoration will see her returned to the state she was in when she tendered to *Titanic* in 1912.

And so ends the story of the most famous shipping line in history, famed for its quality service and luxurious vessels, for its innovations as well as its failures. White Star rose out of the remains of a bankrupt sailing ship line, grew to be one of the most important shipping lines of the twentieth century and escaped bankruptcy again only by a forced merger with its bitter rival Cunard. The merger, of the Government's making, was done to ensure a supply of ships capable of being converted into armed merchant cruisers when or if war came.

Its fate was to die slowly, bitterly even, at the hands of an unsympathetic competitor it had merged with. The line itself has become the stuff of legends, its most infamous vessel also the most famous ship of all time. But White Star was not just *Titanic*, it was a highly successful business, responsible for the transport of million people to the USA, South Africa, Australia and New Zealand with a staff of tens of thousands at its peak and it is for the sixty-odd years of steamship history that it should be remembered for.

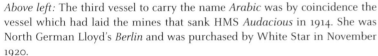

Above left: The third vessel to carry the name *Arabic* was by coincidence the vessel which had laid the mines that sank HMS *Audacious* in 1914. She was North German Lloyd's *Berlin* and was purchased by White Star in November 1920.

Above right: Arabic was used by both White Star and Red Star but she ended her days in White Star's livery. In 1931, she made her last journey to the breakers in Genoa.

Right: In 1921 the American Line's *Haverford* was transferred to White Star and used by them until May 1922, when she transferred back to the American Line.

Opposite: Olympic enters Jarrow on her final voyage..

Above, left and right: Built by Blohm und Voss at Hamburg for the Hamburg Amerika Line, *Bismarck* was, at her launch in 1914, the largest ship in the world. Unfortunately, war started before much of her fitting out could be done and she was laid up for the duration. In June 1919 she was assigned to Britain as war reparation. Fitting out was restarted but a fire in 1920 caused much damage. On 28 March 1922 work was completed and she sailed from Hamburg as *Bismarck*, headed for Southampton. The British government had sold her with her sister *Imperator* to Cunard and White Star, who jointly purchased the vessels.

On 1 April, *Bismarck* commenced her sea trials and is shown here in HAPAG livery on these trials. From there she sailed to Southampton and was renamed *Majestic* on 12 April.

Opposite: Three new ships were built for the Canadian service too, with *Regina* coming first, in Dominion Line colours and with a single funnel. *Pittsburgh* was next The other ship, *Doric*, was launched in 1922 and was only the second turbine ship for White Star.

WHITE STAR LINE.

TRIPLE-SCREW S.S. "PITTSBURGH, 16.322 TONS.

Above: *SS Mobile* in White Star Livery. She joined the fleet in 1920 for a short period.

Left: This colour poster was used to advertise the joint White Star-Dominion Line service to Canada in the early 1920s.

Above left: Majestic in the Ocean Dock with the steam tug *Greetings*. In the early 1920s, the dock was renamed as the Ocean Dock, although it had been built specifically in 1911 for the White Star Line's *Olympic*-class vessels.

Right: By the mid-1920s, White Star was again serving many different parts of the world as this advertising bookmark attests.

Below left: Majestic was fitted with new propellers, manufactured by Stone of Deptford. These huge props powered her to 25kt.

A sectional plan of *Majestic,* used inside a company brochure for the ship.

R·M·S·MAJESTIC

THE WORLD'S LARGEST LINER

WHITE STAR LINE
QUADRUPLE SCREW
R.M.S. MAJESTIC
56,621 TONS
THE WORLD'S LARGEST LINER

4·5 FEET, BEAM 100·15 FEET, DEPTH (FROM KEEL TO BOAT DECK) 101 FEET, AND TONNAGE 56,621. WILL BE SEEN FROM THE DIAGRAMATIC PICTURE OF ITS INTERIOR.

Above left: In 1924 a new floating dry dock was built for the port of Southampton. It was opened by the Prince of Wales and the first ship to use it was the Union Castle Line's RMS *Windsor Castle*, but the dock was large enough to take *Majestic*, which was at the time the largest ship in the world. It took eight hours to berth a ship in the dock and raise it out of the water.

Above right: A superb view of *Majestic* being docked at Southampton in the late 1920s. In 1923 she carried 2,625 passengers on one voyage – a company record.

Opposite page, clockwise from top left: The International Mercantile Marine issued its own magazine. As *Majestic* was the largest ship in the fleet, she often appeared on the cover, this time on the April 1928 issue.

Majestic was the first ocean liner to enter the King George V Graving dock. In the early 1930s, despite the Depression, a whole new extension was built on Southampton's Docks. The new Western Docks also included a huge new graving dock, designed to take the RMS *Queen Mary*, then under construction at Clydebank. In January 1934, *Majestic* was the first ship to sail into the dock for overhaul.

Majestic being berthed in the Ocean Dock, Southampton. In 1934 Cunard and White Star merged. Although, it had a drastic effect on White Star's fleet, much of which was either sold off or scrapped, *Majestic* continued to sail in her old livery.

Clockwise from top right: Miss B.A. Tucker in a scene from the 35mm film *Turning Her Round*. Filmed by the General Post Office Film Unit in 1934, the documentary told the story of *Majestic*'s twenty-four-hour turnaround in Southampton.

Majestic in the Solent, passing some of the many steam and motor yachts always to be found between Cowes and Southampton.

In 1936, after her 207th voyage, *Majestic* was laid up in February at the Western Docks. After only fourteen years service, she was deemed surplus to requirements. In May, she was sold to Thomas W. Ward for scrapping but soon after she was sold again to the Admiralty for use as a cadet ship, the largest they had ever owned. Here, she is seen after the auction of her fixtures and fittings and awaiting final conversion.

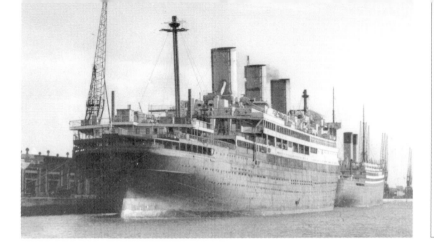

Above left: Converted at a cost of £472,000, *Majestic* was renamed HMS *Caledonia*, a name used on a previous wooden walled training ship located on the Forth at Rosyth. To fit under the Forth Rail Bridge, her masts were cut down and the funnels had their black tops removed. Here, she sits in the Western Docks at Southampton in April 1937, awaiting the journey northwards to Scotland. In front of her is *Laurentic* which had been laid up for the best part of a year, and which was to make a solitary trooping voyage to Palestine in 1936.

Above right: This postcard, of *Majestic* and most likely found on board, was used to advertise the sale of her fittings.

Below left: On 8 April, *Majestic* sailed for the last time under her own power out of Southampton. Here, she sails under the Forth Rail Bridge to her new home.

Below right: HMS *Caledonia* was fitted with seven guns and range-finding control equipment for her new task as an artificer's school. This view shows her at Rosyth, complete with cadets and a Royal Marine band.

WHITE STAR LINE

✦

Scholars' Wonder Cruise

☆

from ... Liverpool, Wednesday, March 30th, to Gibraltar, North Africa & Portugal

◇

returning to Liverpool, Saturday, April 9th.

S.S. "DORIC"   16,500 TONS

INCORPORATED ASSOCIATION OF HEADMASTERS (DIVISION XI.)
Chairman, 1932, Mr. C. W. Pilkington-Rogers, M.A., B.Sc.
Hon. Secretary, Mr. R. L. Ager, M.A.
Hon. Organizer for the Cruise, Mr. F. Hampton.

Above: Doric was similar to Dominion's *Pittsburgh* and was built for the Canadian route. By the time of the Cunard-White Star merger she was being used exclusively for cruising with a winter lay-up at Liverpool.

Left: Doric initiated scholars' cruises for the company and this brochure advertises a trip in 1932 to North Africa.

Below: Regina at Liverpool soon after entering service in March 1922. In 1925 she transferred to White Star and her livery was changed. In 1924 *Regina* carried the first tourist class passengers. Tourist class was seen as a way of filling berths eastbound by selling them to American and Canadian tourists who wanted to go to Europe. She was scrapped by Hughes Bolckow in 1947.

Above: Doric met an unfortunate end at the hands of the Chargeurs Reunis vessel *Formigny*, which rammed her in fog on 5 September 1935 near Cape Finisterre. The P&O liner *Viceroy of India* and the Orient Line's *Orion*, on her shakedown cruise, took of the passengers and *Doric* was sailed to Vigo for temporary repairs and then headed for Tilbury for a survey. Despite her young years, the economic climate of the time meant that she was deemed unrepairable and was broken up on the Usk at Cashmore's yard.

Right: Some of the famous passengers who travelled on board White Star ships in the 1920s.

THE OCEAN FERRY

SOME NOTABLE PASSENGERS ON FAMOUS SHIPS

Top row, left to right: Adele Astaire, American dancer, Majestic; Bernard M. Baruch, financier, and his daughter Rene, Majestic; H. C. Jolly, British golfer, Majestic
Second row, left to right: Hugh Gibson, U. S. representative at the Geneva disarmament conference, Olympic; Hon. Alexander C. Moore, former American Ambassador to Spain, Majestic; John D. Rockefeller, Jr., Majestic; Otto H. Kahn, banker, Majestic
Bottom row, left to right: Dr. Gilbert Grosvenor, president National Geographic Society, of Washington, Homeric; Bishop William Manning, head of New York Episcopal diocese, Majestic; Dr. Menas S. Gregory, alienist, Olympic; Dwight W. Morrow, partner in J. P. Morgan & Co., Olympic

11

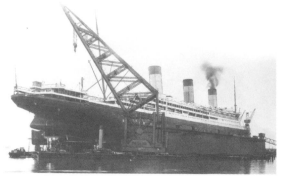

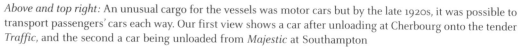

Above and top right: An unusual cargo for the vessels was motor cars but by the late 1920s, it was possible to transport passengers' cars each way. Our first view shows a car after unloading at Cherbourg onto the tender *Traffic,* and the second a car being unloaded from *Majestic* at Southampton

Middle right: Majestic in the floating dry dock in Southampton.

Bottom right: Majestic from Magazine Lane, December 1936. Funnels are cut down and steam is up. Soon, she will be in Rosyth in her new role.

Right and below: Photographed from the *Mauretania* by one of her engineers, *Olympic* is shown in the floating dry dock in Southampton in either 1927 or 1928. Olympic had a major refit which started in December 1927 and it is likely these views date from then.

S.T. "RYDE."

Left and below left: Magnetic, the tender at Liverpool, was built in 1891 by Harland & Wolff and was of 619grt. Equipped for towing, she was used as the passenger tender at Liverpool as well as as a water carrier. In 1925, she was damaged by fire and beached at Tranmere and in December 1932 was sold and renamed as *Ryde*. She travelled to Southampton and was also used locally as a pleasure steamer in Llandudno. In 1935 she was sold for scrap and broken up at Port Glasgow at the same yard that had scrapped the French liner *L'Atlantique*. Another of the Liverpool ships was *Pontic*, used as a water carrier.

Below right: On 10 July 1927, *Adriatic* was the first ship to sail into the new Gladstone Dock in Liverpool only a few hours after it was officially opened by King George V.

Above left: Homeric was another ship purchased from the Shipping Controller in June 1920 and had been the North German Lloyd *Columbus*. Almost completed at the start of the war, she had been laid up at Danzig for the duration. White Star had planned a vessel to be named *Homeric* in 1913 and the *Columbus* took the name. She was intended for a three-ship service to New York with *Olympic* and *Majestic* but proved too slow, despite being the biggest twin-screw reciprocating ship in the world. This view shows her in the Solent.

Above right: Homeric made her last transatlantic crossing in June 1932 and was thereafter sent cruising. She is shown here at Tenerife, where, incidentally, she was damaged at anchor on 28 September 1932 after being rammed by the *Isla de Tenerife* after the smaller ship's steering gear failed as she circled *Homeric*.

Below left: Ready to sail from the Ocean Dock on another cruise, *Homeric* is shown here dressed overall in flags, with *Olympic* berthed behind her. In September 1935, she was laid up at Ryde, Isle of Wight, and sold on 27 February 1936 for scrap. She sailed for Fife and was broken at Inverkeithing. Some of her panelling and part of her grand staircase remains in situ in the Rex Cinema, Argyle Street, Stonehouse, Lanarkshire.

Below right: Albertic was originally intended as the *Munchen* for North German Lloyd but was ceded to Britain and purchased by Royal Mail Lines and named *Ohio*. She was used for their transatlantic service. In February 1927 she transferred to White Star for the astronomical sum of £1M, a paper transaction intended to remove some of the capital and cash from White Star's coffers to feed the debt at the parent company. In July 1934 she was sold for scrap and sailed to Osaka, Japan, for dismantling.

Above: A beautiful passenger list in poster advert style for the Canadian route.

Below left: The last steamship built for White Star was also the only one built on a fixed price contract. She was also the last triple expansion transatlantic liner. She was the *Laurentic* and she is shown here making her maiden arrival into Liverpool on 1 November 1927, dressed overall in flags and carrying guests from Belfast. She sailed on her maiden voyage on 12 November and left for New York, before sailing on the Quebec and Montreal run in April 1928.

Below right: Shown here at Bordeaux, *Laurentic* became a popular cruise ship in the mid-1930s. Only a few weeks after *Doric* was rammed, *Laurentic* too suffered a collision, this time with Blue Star's *Napier Star*. She was repaired and laid up.

Gladstone Dock, Liverpool.

BRITANNIC AND GEORGIC

The last two ships built for White Star were also their only motorships, *Britannic* (III) and *Georgic* (II), which entered service in 1930 and 1932 respectively. In 1928 the keel of a new 60,000grt vessel had been laid and she was to have been *Oceanic* (III) but construction was cancelled after only a few weeks. She would have been a motorship, the largest in the world, and would have looked similar to *Britannic* but with three funnels and four screws. Some of the now redundant steelwork was used in *Britannic*, which was ordered almost immediately after the cancellation of *Oceanic*. As well as being the last White Star ships built, *Britannic* and *Georgic* were also the last Harland & Wolff-built White Star ships, ending a tradition that had started with the first *Oceanic* in 1871.

Above left: This view from October-December 1932 shows *Magnetic* and *Doric* laid up in the Gladstone Dock with the new motorship *Britannic* behind. *Doric* was laid up in October 1932 and *Magnetic* was sold in December 1932 and became the Alexandra Towing Co.'s ST *Ryde*.

Above right: The company's first motorship was the third ship to be named *Britannic* and she was launched on 6 August 1929, making her maiden voyage on 28 June 1930. She was the second-largest motorship to date and was of 26,943grt. The fore funnel was a dummy and contained the radio room at its base. This view, with *Magnetic* tendering, shows her first visit to the Mersey on 21 June 1930.

Above left: Britannic leaving the Landing Stage, Liverpool, in 1930. Her maiden voyage was to New York via Gourock, on the Clyde.

Above right: Britannic was very popular as a cruise ship and is shown here at Monte Carlo.

Below right: From April 1935, *Britannic* sailed from London, via Southampton and Le Havre to New York. This view, dating from mid-1935, shows her in Southampton.

Britannic was of 26,943grt, 683.7ft in length, with a breadth of 82.5ft and had two 10-cylinder diesel engines producing an indicated 13,000hp. Fuel consumption was 88 tons per day and she could do 18kt at 110rpm. She had the squat motorship look so beloved of Harland & Wolff and her forward funnel was a dummy, built to satisfy the eye but serving no useful purpose. It did, however, contain the radio room, engineers' smoke room and water tanks. The ship had eight decks and carried 504 cabin, 551 tourist and 498 third-class passengers. Launched on 6 August 1929, she was only bettered in size by the Italian *Augustus* and was the largest transatlantic motorship. Her interior design was traditional, with a distinct 'country house' feel and ambience while cabin-class was up

The last ship built for White Star before they merged with Cunard was a new sister for *Britannic. Georgic*, the second ship of the name, was an improved version of *Britannic*, with a rounded bridge front and Art Deco interiors. Launched on 12 November 1931, she is shown here in the spring of 1932 at Harland & Wolff's fitting-out basin. In the Thompson graving dock is a Union Castle Line motorship.

to traditional first-class standards and was the largest afloat at the time. Her maiden voyage was from Liverpool via Belfast and the Tail o' the Bank on the Clyde to New York. She performed cruises from New York out of season.

Outwardly similar to *Britannic, Georgic* was launched on 12 November 1931 and was the final White Star ship built. At 27,759grt and 712ft overall she was longer and heavier, with a curved bridge front and no enclosed decks. Her interior, however, was totally unlike that of *Britannic*. Art Deco in style, she was lighter and more modern. Passenger complement was 479 cabin, 557 tourist and 506 third. After eleven days at Liverpool, she left on her maiden voyage on 25 June 1932. On 10 May 1934, she and *Britannic* joined the fleet of the new Cunard White Star Line. In 1935 she joined *Britannic* on the London-Southampton-New York service and was the largest ship to regularly use the Thames.

On 28 August 1939, *Britannic* was called up for service as a troopship and rapidly converted to carry 3,000 soldiers. Her first troopship voyage was in September 1939 from the Clyde to Bombay. Her carrying capacity was later increased to 5,000. *Georgic* remained on the Liverpool-New York run for five complete voyages and was then requisitioned too on 11 March 1940. Converted to carry 3,000 troops on the Clyde, she was used in May to evacuate soldiers from Norway, taking them to Gourock. Immediately after she sailed for Brest and St Nazaire where she assisted in the evacuation of troops and civilians there. She was luckier than Cunard's *Lancastria*, which was bombed at St Nazaire with the loss of upwards of 5,000 lives. *Georgic* was not to escape the German bombers though.

On 22 May 1941, she left the Clyde for Port Tewfik, carrying the 50th Northumberland Division. On 7 July she arrived safely but seven days later was bombed too. Hit twice, she burned and her mid-section was gutted. Beached on the 16th, salvage work started

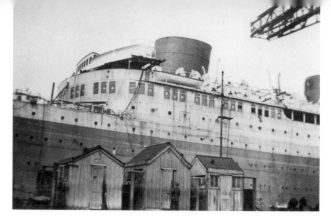

Above left: Georgic dressed in flags at New York, sometime post 1936. Behind her can be seen two funnels of RMS *Queen Mary*.

Above right: Georgic was handed over on 10 July 1932 and arrived on the 12th at Liverpool. Her maiden voyage was on 25 June. She is shown here ready to leave on her maiden voyage, where she sped to New York, arriving a full half-day ahead of schedule. The monument on the left foreground is the Liverpool *Titanic* Memorial.

Middle: Another view of *Georgic* at Belfast, showing her distinctive bridge front. Used for cruising to the Caribbean and Bermuda in the winter season, she was as popular as a cruise ship as she was as a liner.

Below: Georgic in Liverpool in the early 1930s. It was always possible to tell *Georgic* and *Britannic* apart fue to their bridge fronts. *Georgic*'s was curved, while *Britannic*'s was more angular Internally, they were quite different, with *Georgic* being more modern in style..

on 14 September and by 5 December her hulk had been raised and the holes plugged. *Georgic* was towed to Karachi, where she was repaired. She then made her way to Bombay for dry-docking and had a cargo of pig iron loaded. She then sailed for Liverpool and then Belfast where she was rebuilt for further service, losing her dummy funnel and with her forward mast cut down to a stump.

Above left: Both ships were requisitioned during the Second World War and *Georgic* was nearly destroyed while trooping at Port Tewfik on 14 July 1941. Bombed by German aircraft from Greece, she was beached and left to burn out. Salvaged in October, she was made seaworthy at Port Sudan and towed to Karachi for further repairs and then sailed via Bombay for Liverpool. In 1944 she re-emerged, fully rebuilt, as a single-funnelled troopship and served the rest of her war years and into 1947 as a troopship. Shown here at Liverpool, she is most likely repatriating troops back from India

Above right: Although owned by the Ministry of War Transport, *Georgic* was refitted as an emigrant carrier and carried White Star livery from 1949 onwards. She took people of the £10 assisted passage to Australia and New Zealand. Cunard chartered her for numerous seasons on the Liverpool-New York route and she was finally sold for scrapping in January 1956. Arriving at Faslane she was broken by Shipbuilding Industries Ltd, which had also dismantled Cunard's *Aquitania.*

Right: Villefranche in the 1950s, with *Britannic* on a Mediterranean cruise. She made White Star's last ever passenger sailing, leaving New York on 25 November 1960. Her engines were failing and she was destined to sail on 16 December from Liverpool to Inverkeithing, where she too was scrapped.

Meanwhile, *Britannic* had been used as a troopship during the Sicily landings, taking US troops from the USA to Algiers. Her war ended with 180,000 troops carried and a total distance sailed of 376,000 miles. 1946 was spent repatriating troops from the Far East and India. *Georgic*, now owned by the Ministry of War Transport, was also used to repatriate troops through 1946, mainly from India. In 1948, a year after *Britannic*, she was refitted at Palmer's yard at Jarrow, for further use as an emigrant carrier for the ten pound passage to Australia and New Zealand. In between these voyages, she was chartered to Cunard White Star for transatlantic service. On 16 April 1955, she arrived from Japan with British troops and was put up for sale. Her final voyage was from Hong Kong to Liverpool with 800 troops in November 1955 and she was then laid up in December, at Kames Bay, on the Isle of Bute. Her last voyage was to Faslane, where she was broken up in 1956.

Britannic resumed service in 1948 after a refit by Harland & Wolff that took up much of 1947. Her service was from Liverpool via Cobh to New York, with cruises to the Caribbean during the winter. On 1 June 1950 she was involved in a collision with the cargo vessel *Pioneer Land* in the Ambrose Channel. On 11 November 1960 she sailed from New York on her final Cunard voyage, the last ship to fly White Star colours. It was her 275th voyage. Up for sale, she was purchased by British Iron & Steel Co. On 4 December 1960 *Britannic* sailed for Inverkeithing and Thomas W. Ward's shipbreaking yard. In 1961 work started on cutting her up and the last White Star liner disappeared by mid-year. It was a sad end to what was the most famous shipping line and the end vwof an eight-nine year history of the line.

Georgic and *Britannic* had been fantastic ships for White Star and Cunard. They were economical, well-built and designed vessels and popular with crews and passengers alike. Radically different from any other ship that White Star owned, it would have been interesting to see their 60,000grt sister *Oceanic* in service but sadly the Depression and the failure of White Star's then owners, meant that *Oceanic* would never be constructed. Perhaps she would have rivalled that other 1930s icon, Cunard's *RMS Queen Mary*.